HOW YOU CAN BECOME A MILLIONAIRE

Your Lifetime Guide for Building Wealth and Achieving Financial Independence

Ed Dzwonkowski, CFP

Great Spirit Publishing Company
Huntington Beach, California

Great Spirit Publishing Company
P.O. Box 5520
Huntington Beach, CA 92646
www.greatspiritpub.com

This title is available at quantity discounts with bulk purchases for educational, business, or sales promotion use. Contact the publisher for details.

Library of Congress Catalog Card Number: 98-96176

Publisher's - Cataloging-in-Publication
(Provided by Quality Books, Inc.)

Dzwonkowski, Edward.
How you can become a millionaire: your lifetime guide for building wealth and achieving financial independence / Ed Dzwonkowski. -- 1st ed.
p. cm.
Includes bibliographical references.
ISBN 0-9663822-1-8
1. Finance, personal. 2. Saving and investment.
3. Investments. I. Title
HG179.D99 1998 332.024'01
QBI98-455

Printed in the United States of America.

First Edition

10 9 8 7 6 5 4 3 2 1

Book cover design by Digital Canvas.

IMPORTANT NOTICE

The ideas in this book are based on the education and accumulated experience of the author, and they are presented with the intent to generally inform, entertain, and inspire the reader.

The author and publisher believe the information presented in this book would be helpful and should be available to the public, but this book is not sold under the premise that the author and publisher are engaged in rendering legal, accounting, tax, financial planning, investment, or any other professional services, nor do the author and publisher advocate specific securities as investments (expressed or implied). This text should be used only as a general guide and not as your primary resource for making financial decisions.

Investing is not a "get-rich-quick scheme." You must understand that building wealth and becoming financially independent do not happen over night; they happen over time. Furthermore, because there is always risk involved whenever it comes to financial decision-making in general and investing in particular, and because each person is different and each situation unique, the author and publisher urge you the reader to consult with a professional financial advisor before making any financial decisions. It is a sign of wisdom and prudence to seek professional assistance.

Do not use this book if you are not willing to assume all of the risk and accept full and complete personal responsibility for your decisions, actions, and results.

Neither the author nor publisher shall have liability or responsibility to any person or entity for any injury, loss or damage caused, or alleged to be caused, directly or indirectly, by any of the information in this book.

ACKNOWLEDGMENTS

All of the shortcomings and imperfections are entirely mine, but I do want to thank the following outstanding people for taking their editorial pens to this work and making it shine, in much the same way their friendship has brightened my life and made it shine.

Thank you (in alphabetical order) to:

Adon Brownell, a great teacher, and my friend and running partner on the short runs, long runs, and this marathon called life;

Jan Klein, who has been my number one fan and loyal supporter in all of my efforts from the first day we met (as I am hers);

Katherine Morningstar, my fellow student of matters spiritual (we are spiritual beings having a physical experience, not the other way around), who through her wisdom, guidance and example helps me stay centered in faith and trust in our all-knowing, all-powerful, all-loving, all-giving Source;

John Reno, (and Debbie of course), who always provide shelter from the storm by opening their home and their hearts, unconditionally, as only the truest of friends do;

Teacher, counselor, mentor, confidante, friend: whatever I needed, whenever I needed it, these people have always been there at the perfect time, never expecting anything in return. You make all the difference, in my life and in the lives of all whom you touch, and I am deeply grateful.

On a professional note:
I've always believed the Compliance people in securities firms are there to help, not thwart, the efforts of their registered representatives. Thank you, Richard Dunstan, for your help and suggestions.

Thanks also to:
Ron Murphy, who appreciates the "early years" as much as I do while also encouraging me to get through them as quickly as possible, with purpose and integrity; as he has done;
Ruth Sully, whose professional career and personal life is daily proof that success and integrity go hand in hand, and that our work is important and changes lives for the better (despite the frustration and occasional heartache). Thank you for keeping the spark alive in me, and for dragging me along as you lead the charge hill after hill.

Thank you, Blair and Kirsten Larson of Digital Canvas, for going above and beyond the call of duty in designing the beautiful cover which wraps this book. Thank you, Sandy Cox of Webs at Work, for designing the beautiful web site, our home on the Internet. They are magnificent, and so are you.

Lastly, my heartfelt - and I do mean *heartfelt* - thanks to each and every one of my clients, many of whom have also become treasured friends. You are precious. I have been blessed.

DEDICATION

This is the book that I wish my parents could have given to me.

So it's the book I give to my children. And it's the book I give to you, and to your children.

I dedicate this book to the memory of my mom, Connie, who lived the life she wanted to live, but died too soon. She always encouraged me to follow my dreams. Mom, I love you, and I miss you more than I ever imagined I would.

I dedicate this book to my dad (whom everyone knows as "Butch"), who always believed in me, even when I didn't.

I dedicate this book to my wife Terry, and to my children, Nicole, Katie, and Lucy, all of whom I consider to be the richest blessings of my life.

I dedicate this book to all those who have achieved millionaire status, for proving it's possible and for showing us the way.

I also dedicate this book to you and to your quest to become a millionaire, which is the very reason I wrote it.

CONTENTS

Part Two
THE MATHEMATICS OF BECOMING A MILLIONAIRE

Part Three
THE MECHANICS OF BECOMING A MILLIONAIRE

Part Four
THE MAKING OF
A MILLIONAIRE

"Whatever you can do, or dream you can, begin it."

GOETHE

Part One

GETTING ACQUAINTED WITH THE IDEA OF BECOMING A MILLIONAIRE

"MAKE ME A MILLIONAIRE"

As a Certified Financial Planner I've been called upon to assist people from all walks of life to help with their financial planning needs in general and their wealth-building needs in particular. Every person is unique, and everybody's situation is different, and I enjoy the variety and diversity.

On a number of occasions, however, I'll come across someone who says to me:

"Ed, I want you to make me a millionaire."

I reply "I can't make you a millionaire. Only you can do that."

"But I don't know how."

"I'll teach you. The rest is up to you."

"Then teach me."

This book is the teaching. The rest is up to you.

This book is the teaching.

The rest is up to you.

YOU CAN BECOME A MILLIONAIRE

You can become a millionaire, starting from scratch, regardless of who you are, where you are coming from, what you do for a living, how much you earn doing it.

The Millionaire's Club is an all-inclusive club and welcomes anyone as a member, without regard to race, religion, marital status, age, gender, sexual orientation, educational or economic backgrounds. If you look at a roster of the members of The Millionaire's Club, you'll find people with all sorts of abilities and handicaps, from all walks of life.

This should help you understand that you too are welcome to join The Millionaire's Club.

What does it take to become a millionaire?

All you need is a plan, and an undying commitment to stick to that plan. This book offers you an array of plans you can adopt and use as your own, with the flexibility to customize them as you see fit. This book also helps you develop the commitment you need to succeed.

Will this book make you a millionaire? No. Only you can do that. But, you can do it. This book shows you how. This book provides everything you need to know in order to become a millionaire. What you choose to do with this knowledge is, as always, entirely up to you.

All of the current members are looking forward to seeing you join the Millionaire's Club.

What does it take to become a millionaire?

All you need is a plan, and an undying commitment to stick to that plan. This book offers you an array of plans you can adopt and use as your own, with the flexibility to customize them as you see fit. This book also helps you develop the commitment you need to succeed.

MILLIONAIRE MYTHS

Perhaps the reason more people are not millionaires is because of the myths surrounding those who accumulate serious money. Millionaires typically don't flaunt their wealth because they don't want to attract attention to themselves or to their wealth.

It's because of wealthy people's strong desire for privacy that there isn't a lot of widespread public information on what it takes to become a millionaire. As a result, myths develop and circulate, and even get passed down from generation to generation. Lazy people adopt one or more of these myths as their lifetime mantras for staying poor and miserable. The myths are a seemingly valid excuse to justify their financial failures.

Good, ambitious people like you, however, who strive to get ahead, educate themselves about these myths and decide they have no place in their lives.

Let's expose these myths as the barriers to success they truly are.

MYTH #1 You have to have money to make money.

MYTH #2 You have to be smart to become a millionaire.

MYTH #3 The only way to become a millionaire is to marry into money.

MYTH #4 The only way to become a millionaire is to inherit it.

MYTH #5 The only way to become a millionaire is to win the lottery.

MYTH #6 You have to be the CEO of a large corporation, a professional athlete, or an entertainer (in other words: You have to make a lot of money, and/or "be somebody") in order to become a millionaire.

MYTH #7 You have to be ruthless, immoral, or even criminal in order to become a millionaire (in other words: Money is bad, or, You have to be bad to accumulate wealth).

MYTH #8 (Insert your own myth here, just in case it's missing from this list).

Many people have come to believe that the *only* way millionaires become millionaires is through these myths. Indeed, you will find *some* millionaires who became wealthy due to one or more of the above methods, but most millionaires do not rely on these myths to accomplish their goal of financial independence.

Yes, it does take some money and some smarts, but a lot less than you think.

Be a Myth-Blaster. Learn what it takes and follow through with action. Let nothing interfere with your quest to build wealth and achieve financial independence. The truth is, anyone can become a millionaire, including you.

Be a Myth-Blaster. Learn what it takes and follow through with action. Let nothing interfere with your quest to build wealth and achieve financial independence. The truth is, anyone can become a millionaire, including you.

THREE REASONS WHY YOU ARE NOT ALREADY A MILLIONAIRE

REASON #1. You do not know what it takes to become a millionaire.

REASON #2. You know what it takes to become a millionaire but you are not willing to do what it takes.

REASON #3. You know what it takes to become a millionaire and you are willing to do what it takes, but you just haven't gotten around to getting started.

REASON #4. Wait a minute! There are only supposed to be three reasons! There really are only three. Reason #3 is the same as Reason #2. If you haven't started, then you really aren't willing to do what it takes. The end result is the same. The "real" Reason #3, then, is this: you know what it takes to become a millionaire, you are willing to do what it takes, perhaps you have even started doing it, but you do not believe you can become a millionaire.

This book will not only teach you what it takes to become a millionaire, it will also help you believe it is indeed possible for you to become a millionaire. Can a book make it happen for you? No. This must come from you. You are either willing to do what it takes or you are not. You are either going to take the necessary action or you are not.

The choice is yours and yours alone to make. Just as the life you are living today is a result of the choices you made to date, the choices you make today determine the kind of life you will live tomorrow.

Can a book make it happen for you? No. It must come from you.

You are either willing to do what it takes or you are not. You are either going to take the necessary action or you are not.

Just as the life you are living today is a result of the choices you made to date, the choices you make today determine the kind of life you will live tomorrow.

The choice is yours and yours alone to make.

THE MILLIONAIRES CLUB

The IRS estimates that there are more than 3,500,000 millionaires in this country. If you divide this by an estimated population of 260,000,000, it means that better than 1 out of every 100 people in this country is a millionaire.

Look around you carefully. Chances are good someone you know is a millionaire. Perhaps it's a neighbor, co-worker, or even a relative of yours.

The majority of millionaires are not who you think they are (big houses, expensive cars, flashy clothes and jewelry, country club membership, kids in private schools, etc.). Oh no, your typical millionaire does not flaunt it. Your typical millionaire does not advertise the fact that he or she is a millionaire. In fact, just the opposite. Your typical millionaire is very unassuming and lives very modestly. Chances are greater you'd bump into a millionaire and never know it.

Your typical millionaire is more than likely a "self-made" millionaire, having risen from modest means, is still working, happily married, with children, living in the same modest house they've lived in for years, driving modest cars, concerned about and active in the community, etc. They're just normal, average people. The only thing that sets a millionaire apart from their non-millionaire neighbor is their net worth.

There are even more millionaires running around this country than the number provided by the IRS. For some reason the IRS estimate only includes people between the ages of fifty and sixty-four. When you expand the age category to include people older than age sixty-four, and younger than age fifty, the actual total number of millionaires in this country must be substantially higher.

Even with just three-and-a-half-million millionaires, you can see that The Millionaires Club is a rather large club - with members in all 50 states. Contrary to popular belief, membership in The Millionaires Club is open to everyone.

Membership in the Millionaires Club is open to YOU.

Your typical millionaire is more than likely a "self-made" millionaire, having risen from modest means, is still working, happily married, with children, living in the same modest house they've lived in for years, driving modest cars, concerned about and active in the community, etc. They're just normal, average people.

Membership in the Millionaires Club is open to YOU.

JOIN THE CLUB

What are you waiting for? An engraved invitation? Then consider this your engraved invitation:

We, the current members of The Millionaires Club, hereby extend to you an open invitation to join the Club.

It is our strongest desire that you join us. We'd be delighted to have YOU as a member at your earliest convenience.

The only qualification for membership in The Millionaires Club is that you accumulate a million dollars of wealth.

We are in a growth mode and are continually striving to expand our membership. As such, we are always looking for new members. We would be most grateful if you would extend this invitation to your family members and friends.

This invitation is good for the rest of your life (it only expires when you do).

The current members of the Millionaires Club extend to you an open invitation to join the Club.

HOW YOU CAN BECOME A MILLIONAIRE IN FIVE STEPS

They are the same five steps you would take to accomplish anything else in your life.

STEP #1. Set Your Goal. Many people dream of becoming a millionaire, but relatively few people become millionaires. The difference between dreamer/non-achievers and achievers can be summed up in one word: GOALS. The difference between non-achievers and achievers is that non-achievers float aimlessly through life wishing and dreaming and hoping, but rarely doing anything about their dreams (like taking action), while achievers set goals and do something about them (like taking action). If you really truly want to become a millionaire in this lifetime, you must consciously decide you're going to do what it takes to become a millionaire. You must decide you are going to convert your dream into a goal. You set "Becoming a Millionaire" as one of your lifetime goals.

STEP #2. Create Your Plan. The way you convert a dream into a goal is by creating a plan to achieve your goal. Some goals in life are easier to achieve than others. Lifetime goals require a series of subgoals and you incorporate these subgoals into your plan. If you want to become a millionaire in twenty years, where do you need to be in five years? Where should you be in one year? What do you need to do this month, this week, today? Your plan is your strategy for achieving your subgoals, and ultimately your lifetime goal. Continue reading this book and you will soon have enough information to formulate your own plan for becoming a millionaire.

STEP #3. Follow Your Plan. Once you've set your goal and created your plan, you then begin to follow your plan. This sets your goal into motion You begin to see immediate results and this motivates you further. This is very exhilarating! Every step you take brings you closer and closer to your goal! Again, taking action is what separates the achievers from the non-achievers. This has always been the achiever's motto: "Just Do It."

STEP #4. Chart Your Progress. The results you experience will influence your future course of action. Because your results are measurable they enable you to chart your progress, to compare your results with where you expect to be at a certain point of time. Monitoring results for your short-term goals will tell you if you're on track or not for the longer-term goals. If you are achieving your short-term goals you will ultimately achieve your long-term goals.

STEP #5. Modify Your Plan (if necessary). And if you're not on track and are missing the mark, you will simply adjust your course accordingly. Plans are created to be followed, but the very nature of plans dictates that they need modification. As you drive down a new and unfamiliar road, you will be using your map (which is your plan) because you trust and believe that your map will guide you successfully to your destination.

But "stuff happens" that never appeared on the map, and indeed anything can happen as you're driving down your road. Your vehicle may not perform as expected. Perhaps it will even break down and require repair, or complete replacement. There could be obstacles on the road which require unplanned detours.

Some of this stuff may actually be good! Perhaps your replacement vehicle turns out to be much faster than your original! Perhaps your detour turns out to be a shortcut!

Some of this stuff you can control and some you can't. But you always control your plan. No matter what happens along your journey, all you need to do is modify your plan accordingly and keep on keeping on.

The difference between non-achievers and achievers is that achievers set goals and take action on those goals.

If you really truly want to become a millionaire, you must consciously decide you're going to do what it takes to become a millionaire, and then do it.

THE 4 M's OF BECOMING A MILLIONAIRE

In addition to the 5 Steps, it takes 4 M's to become a millionaire.

MATH. If you can count, you can become a millionaire. When you get right down to it, money is nothing more than math. Math, music, and money are all universal languages. Money was invented by people as a means of facilitating trade. Money is nothing more than a universal means by which we can keep score. Keeping score involves counting, so you do need to understand a little bit of math in order to become a millionaire. It's perfectly acceptable to use pencil and paper. You can even use a calculator! Or a computer!

MECHANICS. You need to learn the mechanics of money in order to become a Millionaire. The mechanics of money involves applying simple mathematical concepts to real money. You specifically need to learn how money grows in the "real" world, and you will learn this in Part Three of this book. You will learn what to do with *your* money in order to make it grow all the way into a million dollars, to enable you to become a Millionaire.

MONEY. It takes money to become a millionaire. Yes, it will take some of your own money to become a millionaire. But not a lot, comparatively speaking. Certainly not as much as you may imagine. Believe it or not you can start from scratch, with absolutely nothing in the bank, and still become a millionaire. This assumes you have some time, and most people do seem to have more time than they have money. Time is your greatest ally. The more time you have (meaning the sooner you start), the less of your own out-of-pocket money it will take to become a millionaire. This will make more sense to you once you understand the math, and suffice it to say you will be surprised and amazed at how relatively little money it takes to become a millionaire once you get started and stick with it.

MOTIVATION. You will not become a millionaire merely because you know *How You Can Become A Millionaire.* You must apply what you know, using your knowledge and using your money. You must have the desire to become a Millionaire, and then you must act on that desire. Applying the knowledge and taking action is what distinguishes the wishful Millionaires from the actual Millionaires. Do you have the motivation to get started and stick with it (no matter how long it takes)?

Think of the 4 M's as the cornerstones in the foundation of your lifetime goal to build wealth and become a Millionaire. It's time to break ground, dig in, and start building.

Once you learn what to do with your money to make it grow, you will be surprised and amazed at how relatively little money it takes to become a millionaire once you get started and stick with it.

Part Two

THE MATHEMATICS OF BECOMING A MILLIONAIRE

THE MOST POWERFUL WEALTH-BUILDING TOOL IN THE UNIVERSE

The genius Albert Einstein is reported to have described it as the Eighth Wonder of the World. He was talking about the Miracle of Compounding. Compounding is a mathematical concept which has practical considerations in "real life." Compounding is a major force in helping you to become a millionaire so you should become familiar with it immediately.

One dictionary defines compounding as: to increase by an amount that itself increases. Compounding allows your money to grow "all by itself," without you having to do anything else. Has anyone in your life ever said "What, do you think money grows on trees?" Wouldn't it be wonderful if money did grow on trees? Compounding is like money growing on trees.

You start out with an amount of money that you want to put to work for you. This is like planting the seed for your money tree. You do need to plant it in a place where it'll get the necessary nourishment to grow. If you've done it right, it'll start to grow immediately. In the beginning, however, it's just a seedling. Perhaps it just appears and you wonder if it'll ever survive. It might even be tempting to give up - pull it up and throw it away. But you continue to watch it and protect it and tend to it, and as time goes on it grows larger and stronger and one day you realize that your little apple seed has grown into a mighty tree. Moreover, your tree has provided you with a never-ending supply of delicious fruit and a multitude of additional seeds, year after year after year.

HOW MONEY GROWS

Let's do the math on Compounding. Let's call the seed you plant *principal*, and let's call the growth of your seed the *interest* you earn on your principal. Let's say you start out with $100 in principal and you plant it in a place where your $100 can earn 10% a year. At the end of your first year your $100 is worth $110 ($100 plus 10%). You leave your $110 to continue growing and at the end of the second year it's worth $121 ($110 plus 10%). You leave your $121 to continue growing and at the end of the third year it's worth $133 ($121 plus 10%). Look at the numbers in The Miracle of Compounding table.

You will have doubled your money by the end of Year 8, tripled it by the end of Year 12, and quadrupled it by the end of Year 15. In twenty-five years you will have multiplied your money ten-fold. In twenty-five years your money will have grown to ten times the amount you started with. You started with only $100 and never contributed another dime of principal, but in twenty-five years you have more than $1,000.

The reason for the growth - the doubling, tripling, ten-fold increases - is because your interest grows on top of interest. It's money piling on top of money. You kicked off the pile with your $100 but the earnings grew on both principal *and* on all of the interest year after year.

What if you planted other $100 seeds throughout the months and years? You'd have little money trees growing all over the place, all worth varying amounts but all worth substantially more than the original $100 seeds. Best of all, they keep growing and growing more valuable with each passing year.

Imagine yourself looking out over a large piece of undeveloped land. Now imagine a large orchard of sturdy trees, abundantly producing juicy, delicious fruit not just for one season, but month after month, year after year, supplying you and your heirs with all the fruit you'll need for the rest of your lives.

This orchard can be yours some day.

Only you can plant the seeds. You can do it one seed at a time, one tree at a time.

Start planting today.

Wouldn't it be wonderful if money did grow on trees?

Compounding is like money growing on trees.

Start planting today, and an orchard can be yours some day.

The Miracle of Compounding

Starting with a one-time deposit of $100 and growing it at 10% a year, this table demonstrates the amazing effect of the Miracle of Compounding.

Starting Value	Plus 10%	New Value	at End of Year
$100	$10	$110	1
$110	$11	$121	2
$121	$12	$133	3
$133	$13	$146	4
$146	$15	$161	5
$161	$16	$177	6
$177	$18	$195	7
$195	$19	$214	8
$214	$21	$236	9
$236	$24	$259	10
$259	$26	$285	11
$285	$29	$314	12
$314	$31	$345	13
$345	$35	$380	14
$380	$38	$418	15
$418	$42	$459	16
$459	$46	$505	17
$505	$51	$556	18
$556	$56	$612	19
$612	$61	$673	20
$673	$67	$740	21
$740	$74	$814	22
$814	$81	$895	23
$895	$90	$985	24
$985	$98	$1,083	25
$1,083	$108	$1,192	26

YOUR EASY PAYMENT PLAN FOR BECOMING A MILLIONAIRE

Here in America we have Easy Payment Plans for just about everything. You can buy a car, a computer, a stereo, a refrigerator, and a couch on an Easy Payment Plan. These Easy Payment Plans are advertised every day of the year in every state in the Union. No payments until July! No interest for the first 90 days!

Once you factor in the interest and the length of time you'll be making payments, you're likely to be paying 18% to 22% more for an item which is worth a fraction of its original value by the time you own it free and clear. It may be a terrible transaction for you the consumer, but it *is* easy!

Well, believe it or not, we have an Easy Payment Plan for becoming a millionaire. Not many people are aware of this. These plans are never advertised anywhere. Yet they are a terrific deal for you the consumer! And they *are* easy.

It doesn't cost you a dime of interest, *ever*. You can start and stop payments whenever you like. You can change the amount of your payment whenever you wish. No one will ever come and take away your purchases if you fail to live up to your end of the deal. The payments are surprisingly affordable. Best of all, by the time you finish making your payments, your purchases are worth substantially *more* than when you started.

I wonder if you know just how easy it is to become a millionaire. If somebody told you that you could become a millionaire by saving $61 a week, would you be interested? Could you come up with the $61 a week? If not immediately, then eventually? Would you do it?

Let me be the somebody to tell you. All it takes to become a millionaire is socking away $61 a week - that's $264 a month - earning 10% a year on your money, for 35 years.

Look at the two schedules which follow. Choose your own Millionaire Easy Payment Plan and design your own plan for becoming a millionaire.

The first plan shows you how long it will take to become a millionaire given a particular monthly investment in round dollars. The second plan shows you what your weekly and monthly investment must be to achieve your goal within a certain time frame.

Earning 10% a year...

You'll be a millionaire in 58 years if you save $ 25 a month.
You'll be a millionaire in 45 years if you save $ 100 a month.
You'll be a millionaire in 35 years if you save $ 264 a month.
You'll be a millionaire in 25 years if you save $ 754 a month.
You'll be a millionaire in 20 years if you save $1,317 a month.
You'll be a millionaire in 10 years if you save $4,882 a month.

By the way: cars, computers, refrigerators, stereos, and couches eventually break down and need repair, become worn out or obsolete, and sooner or late (usually sooner than later) get thrown out as they need to be replaced. All of these items lose their value and are worth a fraction of their original cost in a very short period of time. Yet most people have a number of easy payment plans going at any given point in time, and when you add it all up you see they have easy payment plans going their entire lives.

Wealth does not break down or need repair. Wealth does not become worn out or obsolete. Wealth does not get thrown out, nor does it need to be replaced. Wealth, invested properly, *grows* in value over time and is worth far greater than when originally invested. Wealth can last forever and be enjoyed by generations.

Wealth provides the means to buy all the comforts and luxuries life has to offer.

Given the choice, which would you prefer to put on an easy payment plan?

Become a lifetime member of The Millionaire's Club. All it takes is $264 a month. That's $61 a week.

(Note: When I talk about earning 10% a year on payments which are made monthly, which I do repeatedly throughout the book, the actual annual rate that is earned is slightly higher than 10%. This is due to the cumulative effect of the Miracle of Compounding at work on each monthly payment made throughout the entire year, which is greater than the Miracle of Compounding at work on a lump sum payment made once a year. For the sake of simplicity I stick with an even 10% in all discussions and examples).

I wonder if you know just how easy it is to become a Millionaire.

Here in America we have Easy Payment Plans for just about everything. Believe it or not, we have an Easy Payment Plan for becoming a Millionaire.

Millionaire Easy Payment Plan

This plan shows you how long it will take to become a millionaire given a specific monthly investment, earning 10% a year.

Monthly Investment	Years Required*
$25	58
$50	52
$100	45
$150	41
$200	38
$250	36
$300	34
$350	32
$400	31
$450	30
$500	29
$750	25
$1,000	23
$1,500	19
$2,000	17
$2,500	15
$5,000	10
$7,500	6
$12,000	5

* rounded to nearest whole number

Millionaire Easy Payment Plan

This table shows you what your specific weekly and monthly investment must be, given a particular time goal, earning 10% a year.

Years Desired	Weekly Investment	Monthly Investment
60	$4.90	$21.23
50	$13.32	$57.72
45	$22.02	$95.40
40	$36.49	$158.13
35	$60.78	$263.39
30	$102.09	$442.38
25	$173.92	$753.67
20	$303.92	$1,317.00
15	$556.78	$2,412.72
10	$1,126.56	$4,881.74
5	$2,980.09	$12,913.71

A WORD OF ENCOURAGEMENT

Now that you've spent a little time analyzing the information in the Millionaire Easy Payment Plans perhaps your emotions are swirling. You may be feeling euphoric. Yes, you *can* become a millionaire! You understand it's simply a matter of math. You see the numbers in black and white. You know the numbers in your own life, and you firmly believe you can make the numbers work in your life.

In contrast, perhaps you're feeling a little disappointed, maybe even depressed. Now that the numbers have been laid out, maybe they're not what you expected. Odds are you were secretly hoping it wouldn't take that long to become a millionaire. Maybe there's a little voice inside of your head right now that's saying something like "thirty-five years! I figured there was a catch. All this millionaire talk sounded too good to be true. Thirty-five years is forever. I could be dead in thirty-five years!"

Let me tell you something. That little voice has held you back from so much good in your life, and it will hold you back on your Millionaire dream if you let it. That little voice is negative, pessimistic, and downright ugly. It's the result of the negative conditioning to which we've all been exposed throughout our lives. Stop playing those negative tapes immediately.

CHANGE YOUR TAPE

There's a positive voice inside of you too, much larger and far more powerful than the feeble, whining, negative little voice. It's the voice which speaks from your heart, the place where you harbor your dreams. It believes in you and helps you succeed, if you let it. Call out this positive voice and have a different conversation with yourself.

Stop playing those negative tapes. Eject them, erase them, and record new ones. Replace the negative self-defeating tapes with life-enriching positive tapes. It's all a matter of perspective. If you think something is possible for you, you're right. If you think something is impossible for you, you're right. Change your perspective.

What if you *weren't* dead in thirty-five years? How old will you be? You'll be the same age whether you're a millionaire or not! Take a long, hard look at your life. Ask yourself this question: Given the choice, would you rather be a millionaire, or in the same financial position you are in today?

Unless you initiate a change in your life, you will *automatically* be in the same financial position you are in today. This is the default setting, mandated by the Law of Inertia: if you continue doing the same things you're doing today, you'll end up in the same position you are in today. To change your future, you must change what you're doing today.

Don't obsess on the fact that it takes 35 years. Thirty-five years will fly by quicker than you can blink and spit. (Ask anyone who's lived for at least 35 years). If you plan to be around in 35 years, wouldn't you prefer to be a millionaire? You're going to be 35 years older anyway, why not also be a millionaire?

Forget about the 35 years. Focus on the million dollars. Focus on *your* million dollars.

Perhaps, instead, your negative voice is saying things like *this* to you: "How am I going to come up with $264 a month? I'm barely making ends meet as it is. Every time I try to save a little money something always comes up and wipes me out. I never seem to get ahead. Maybe I could scrape together $25 a month, maybe even a hundred in a good month, but $264 every month? Forget it!"

I'm going to be tough with you right now. Knowing that $264 a month means the difference between becoming a millionaire and not becoming a millionaire, and you're *really* struggling with this question, then you do not have what it takes to become a millionaire. You do belong in the Millionaire's Club, but you'll never make it. Sorry to be so blunt but it is the truth. Face the truth and go in peace. (Finish the book anyway - there's lots of other information you might find useful. And who knows, maybe you'll even change your mind!)

THE ONES THAT MAKE IT USE POSSIBILITY THINKING

The ones that make it to the Millionaire Club may have had those same negative thoughts at first. But they have a different conversation with themselves. They want to become a millionaire so badly they're willing to do whatever it takes to achieve it. They're grateful for this wonderful, new understanding that all it takes is $264 a month to become a millionaire. They're figuring out how to do it in less than thirty-five years. They're playing with numbers in their mind: "Let's see, if I do this and that, it'll get me to X dollars a month and all I'll need to get to $264 is another X dollars a month. In a few years, I bet I can even increase it from $264 a month and get there even sooner. Wow, I can do it!"

They're exploring the possibilities and forging a way to achieve the goal. They start with what they *can* do, and they build from there. Even if it takes some time. Even if it takes some effort, and anything worth having in this life almost always requires some effort. If others can find a way to make it happen, why can't you?

So the question to ask yourself instead is this: is it worth scraping together $61 a week knowing it will make you a millionaire in time? If you don't have $264 a month to start - how much do you have to start?

What happens if you fall short of the goal? If for one reason or another you did not make it to the million-dollar mark, could you make do with a half million? A quarter million? In thirty-five years you may end up with a few thousand dollars to your name. Or you just might manage to accumulate $100,000 or $250,000 or $500,000. You might even be a millionaire.

The decisions you make today, and along the way, will determine your results. The choice is entirely yours. No one will do it for you. No one cares as much about your future as you do. Dare to dream big. Yes, you *can* become a millionaire. You deserve to become a millionaire.

The sooner you get started, the sooner you will arrive.

A SPECIAL NOTE FOR PARENTS, GRANDPARENTS, AUNTS, UNCLES, AND OTHER GOOD FRIENDS.

Imagine what your life would be like today if only someone you loved and respected had sat you down at the age of 13, or 16, or 20, or 30, and taught you how you could become financially independent by simply putting aside a small amount of money each month and growing it for the future.

If someone had done this for you, what difference would it have made in your life today?

Do you know much a typical teenager spends on junk food, the latest music, "stylish" clothes? Can you find a 15-year-old to show him or her how $13.39 a week (earning 10% a year) will turn into a million dollars by age 65? Can you explain how they can reach the goal sooner by increasing the amount of their monthly savings? Can you encourage them to make a commitment and make it as easy as possible for them to stick with it?

What about people you know in their twenties and thirties? Who do you really like or love so much that that you hope becomes financially independent? Can you find the time to share some of the valuable information in this book? Perhaps you could give the book as a gift, with your own handwritten inscription of encouragement in the front. Offer (with excitement and enthusiasm!) to make yourself available to discuss it with them later. Follow up with them in a week or two, and again on their birthday. Be lovingly persistent. One person can make a difference. Why shouldn't it be you?

When a new baby is born into your family, you know how people like to help the new parents buy clothes, toys, and nursery items. Dare to be bold and unique. Set yourself apart. Establish a Financial Independence account for this new important person in your life. Starting from the day a child is born, $8.08 a week ($35 a month), earning 10% a year, would make him or her a millionaire by the age of 55, and $264 a month would do it by age 35.

My special appeal to parents, grandparents, aunts, uncles, and other good friends is this: why not give a precious child or young adult the head start you didn't receive? Don't worry about not being able to maintain a long-term commitment. Just getting it started is the greatest gift of all. Take that first important step. Focus only on one step at a time, and complete that step before even beginning to think about taking the next step. Involve others and make it a team effort.

We all would like to make a positive contribution to the world at large, and especially to change someone's life for the better in particular. This is your opportunity to make a difference. A BIG difference. Seize the opportunity.

ANNE'S STORY

Anne Scheiber worked as an auditor for the IRS for 23 years. Poring over peoples' tax returns all those years, she came to the conclusion that the way to become wealthy is to save your money and make it grow by investing it. Starting with $5,000 she scraped together in 1944 and adding as much as she could over the years, she ended up with TWENTY MILLION DOLLARS by the time she died in 1995, at the age of 101.

Money Magazine reported that as she approached age 90, Anne Scheiber's investments were generating $40,000 in income to her. Oh, by the way, that's $40,000 a MONTH! That's right, her portfolio was generating an income of nearly a half a million dollars a year. By the time she died it was generating three quarters of a million dollars a year ($62,500 a month). Can you live on $750,000 a year each and every year? If you fell short of the mark, could you possibly survive on $40,000 a month?

Anne Scheiber first came to national attention when it was announced that she left almost all of her money to Yeshiva University in New York City. *Money* Magazine, which did a cover story on her in January 1996, also said "Given Anne's performance, it is not unreasonable to think that 25-year-olds with $5,000 today who follow her example could amass a multimillion-dollar portfolio by age 65."

Anne Scheiber did not become a multimillionaire by marrying into money (she never married). She did not inherit her money (she was one of nine children whose father died when she was a teenager, forcing her mother to work to support the family). She did not become a multimillionaire by winning the lottery, or as the CEO of a large corporation, as a professional athlete, as an entertainer, or by living a life of crime. No, Anne became a multimillionaire simply by saving and investing her money, year after year, one year at a time. She was an ordinary person who put the Miracle of Compounding to work for her and achieved extraordinary results.

Do you think 50 years old is too late to get started on saving and investing your money? Anne Scheiber was 50 years old when she started. Do you think 35 years is too long to have to keep investing to reach a goal? Anne Scheiber invested regularly for 51 years.

If Anne could do it, then so can you!

Imagine what your life would be like today if only someone you loved and respected had sat you down at the age of 13, or 16, or 20, or 30, or 50, and taught you how you could become financially independent by simply putting aside a small amount of money each month and growing it for the future.

Do you think 50 years old is too late to get started on saving and investing your money? Do you think 35 years is too long to have to keep investing to reach a goal?

Given the choice, would you rather be a millionaire, or in the same financial position you are in today? If you keep doing the same things you're doing today, you're going to keep getting the same results.

And if you fell short of the goal, could you make do with a half million? A quarter million? A tenth of a million?

The sooner you get started, the sooner you will arrive.

THE MIRACLE IN ACTION

You know that that setting aside $264 a month, earning 10% a year, for 35 years will make you a millionaire. If you multiply 35 years times 12 months per year you'll get a total of 420 months. Multiply the 420 months times $264 a month and you get $110,880. Let's round it up and call it $111,000.

So, all you will have had to actually part with all those years was some $111,000. Yet you've now got a million dollars. Subtract this $111,000 from a million dollars and you get $889,000. Where does the rest of the million dollars come from?

The other $889,000 that makes up your million all came from the growth of your savings: the earning 10% a year on your monthly investments. You turn your total out-of-pocket investment of $111,000 into a million dollars. The money you actually had to work for and put into the till was a mere 11% of the total million. The other $889,000 - 89% of the million - came entirely from your money working for you.

This is the Miracle of Compounding and is the greatest math lesson of your life. Understanding the Miracle of Compounding and actively, aggressively applying it in your life can make the difference between poverty and prosperity. Believe in miracles! The Miracle of Compounding can make you a millionaire!

The Miracle of Compounding is the greatest math lesson of your life. Understanding the Miracle of Compounding and actively, aggressively applying it in your life can make the difference between poverty and prosperity. Believe in miracles! The Miracle of Compounding can make you a millionaire!

A MILLIONAIRE'S GREATEST ALLY

Your greatest ally as a "Millionaire in the Making" is Time. Considering that the majority of people seem to have more time than they have money, this is a good thing!

Time works on your behalf. It is your greatest ally. The sooner you start, the less monthly investment it takes to achieve the goal and become a millionaire. The longer you put your money to work for you the more your money will grown and the less you will have to part with out of pocket.

Let's look at the Greatest Ally table. If you started investing $264 a month at age 20 and kept it up until age 65, earning 10% a year, your money would grow to $2,767,380. Yet all you actually parted with throughout the years was $142,560. In other words you contributed , out of your own pocket, $3,168 a year for 45 years, to get to $142,560. The difference between your ending value and your out-of-pocket contribution is $2,339,700, representing the growth of your money due to the Miracle of Compounding. In this instance it is 95% of the ending value!

Obviously the less time you have to invest, the smaller the ending value. More importantly, the less time you invest, the smaller the percentage of your ending value will be attributed to growth. At age 20, your out-of-pocket contribution is a mere 5% of the ending value. At age 30, your out-of-pocket contribution represents 11%; at age 40, 23%, at age 50, 43%; and at age 60, with only 5 years of growth, 77%.

Let's look at the same table another way. **If you start at age 30, you'd be a millionaire at age 65**. If you waited ten years to get started, you'd accumulate a mere one-third of that million (but wouldn't it be nice to have $350,000?) Waiting until you're fifty to get started reduces your ending value to about a tenth of a million dollars (but even so, more than half of it comes from the growth of your investments - less than half of it comes out of your pocket). Starting at age 60 only gives you five years of growth and you end up with $20,000 which is only 2% of a million dollars. (Nonetheless, starting at age 60 is better than not starting at all, and you've still got many good years ahead of you).

If, however, you started at age 20, you'd be worth more than two-and-a-half million dollars at age 65!

If you are in your 40's, 50's, 60's, 70's, and beyond, time is still very much in your side. It is never too late to set a goal and commit to achieving it. Make a solemn vow to yourself that you will *never* use your age as an excuse to fail. It's not over until you've breathed your last breath. Treat today, and every day going forward, as the first day of your new financial life. Armed with new tools and new knowledge, you may truly celebrate the dawning of a new era in your life.

If your 20's and 30's *are* behind you as you read this, and you want to make a positive contribution to the world at large, and change someone's life for the better in particular, find someone in their teens, 20's, or 30's and share this information with them. Then check in with them periodically to keep them motivated. (This keeps you motivated too)!

Time is your greatest ally. Team up with your greatest ally, climb your Millionaire Mountain, conquer it, and achieve your Millionaire goal. Time is on your side. Use it to the best advantage. Start saving and growing your money immediately.

Time is your greatest ally. Team up with your greatest ally. Start saving immediately. Make a solemn vow to yourself that you will never use your age as an excuse to fail. It's not over until you've breathed your last breath.

Time is Your Greatest Ally

This table shows you how your money grows over time, investing $264 a month, earning 10% a year.

Starting Age	Value at Age 25	Value at Age 35	Value at Age 45	Value at Age 55	Value at Age 65
20	20,443	109,420	350,284	1,002,312	2,767,380
30	-	20,443	109,420	350,284	1,002,312
40	-	-	20,443	109,420	350,284
50	-	-	-	20,443	109,420
60	-	-	-	-	20,443

		Total at Age 65 attributed to...	
Starting Age	Value at Age 65	...out of pocket	...and to growth
20	2,767,380	142,560	2,624,820
30	1,002,312	110,880	891,432
40	350,284	79,200	271,084
50	109,420	47,520	61,900
60	20,443	15,840	4,603

A MILLIONAIRE'S TWO WORST ENEMIES

If you accept time as your greatest ally then you will have no trouble understanding that Procrastination is one of your two worst enemies. It is the biggest reason people fail to accumulate significant amounts of money over the course of their lives. It's the "too little, too late" syndrome. People wait too long to start saving, and by the time they do start they typically cannot afford to set aside as much as is required to reach their desired goals.

Compare two investors and their results at age 65. Investor #1, age 36, invests $2,000 a year for 10 years, and stops completely, never investing another dime beyond the total $20,000 invested. Investor #2 procrastinates for those first 10 years and waits until age 46 when he begins investing $2,000 a year. He keeps investing all the way up to age 65, for a total of 20 years and $40,000. Both investors earn the same average annual rate of return of 10% on their investments.

At age 65, Investor #1 has an ending value of $235,879 on original contributions of $20,000, but Investor #2 only ends up with $126,005 on his original contributions of $40,000. Despite that Investor #2 **invested twice as much money, for twice as long, he never caught up** with Investor #1! Investor #1 invested half as much money, and even stopped investing when Investor #2 was only getting started, and still he ended up with $109,874 more money than Investor #2! (Source: The AIM IRA: *A Cornerstone for Your Retirement Savings Program*).

The "Penalty for Procrastination" table which follows further illustrates this point. You can see from the above example and from the table that the sooner you start, the less out of your own pocket it's going to take and the larger your ending value will be. The earlier compounding begins, the more your money will grow. Procrastination has a stiff penalty attached to it. It is too high a price to pay. A bad case of procrastination can make the difference between poverty and prosperity. The best part about this particular enemy is that the enemy is you! You can fight this enemy single-handedly, and win every time. Don't Delay! Start Saving Today!

YOUR OTHER FORMIDABLE ENEMY

Your second greatest enemy is Taxes. We rely on our federal, state, and local governments to provide a wide array of services for us, and we fund our governments and pay for those services via tax dollars. For example, we pay sales taxes, real estate taxes, estate transfer and inheritance taxes, and of course income taxes. When we pay taxes on our income, every year we add up our total income for the year and our income taxes are based on this total. The total includes your wages, and it includes investment income. Any money you receive throughout the year from your savings and investments will be included in your total income for the year and you will be taxed on it.

As you save and invest your money it will grow over time. In all of our math examples we have been counting on it to grow 10% a year. This 10% growth will come from interest and dividend income you earn, and it will come from capital gains. A capital gain is the profit you make on an investment, by selling it at a higher price than you paid for it. We'll discuss this in greater detail in later chapters but the point to make for now is that the government will get a piece of all of your efforts, including the income you receive as wages and salary, the income you receive on your investments, and the profits you experience on the growth in value of your investments.

In other words, taxes are going to cut in on your targeted 10% growth every year, effectively reducing this 10% to a substantially lower number. If you start out with $1,000 and earn 10% you will have earned $100. Let's say you pay $28 in taxes on your $100 earnings. This leaves you with a net of $72. You're effectively only earning $72 on your $1,000 investment which translates into 7.2% a year.

Growing your money at 7.2% a year is very different from growing it at 10% a year, and over time this difference is extraordinary. Looking at the table on the next page your $264 a month earning 10% a year for 35 years will result in more than a million dollars. At 7.2% a year for 35 years, in contrast, your $264 a month will only result in $498,756, which is **less than half of your desired goal.** Even if you took the entire million dollars (earned at the 10% rate) in a lump sum and then paid the same 28% in taxes you were paying all along via the reduced rate of 7.2%, you would still end up with nearly $223,000 more money.

The difference is due to the tax bite: not only are your out-of-pocket savings contributions growing at a lower rate, but so are all of the cumulative earnings on your savings growing at a lower rate. As we've just seen, over the course of 35 years, the cumulative effect is substantial.

Taxes are your second worst enemy. Unlike Procrastination, Taxes won't mean the difference between poverty and prosperity, but they can mean the difference between becoming a millionaire or not.

There is good news, though. The government doesn't want the responsibility or burden of taking care of us in old age so it encourages us to save and invest our money so we can take care of ourselves later in life. The government calls this stage of life "retirement" and says we can reach it at age 59-1/2. The government says that if we tell it we're saving for retirement, then we don't have to pay any taxes on our investments, for all the years we're saving for retirement, until it comes time for us to begin living off of our investments. So the government helps us fight the enemy by allowing us to protect the earnings and growth of our money from taxation, for all the years our money is growing, as long as we agree not to tap into it until we are ready to retire. This is great leverage for fighting the enemy!

We'll get into this in greater detail in the *Tax-Advantaged Investing* chapter, but the point for now is that Taxes and Procrastination are your worst enemies, and they can prevent you from becoming a millionaire.

Procrastination has a stiff penalty attached to it. It is too high a price to pay. A bad case of procrastination can make the difference between poverty and prosperity.

We have seen the enemy, and it is us.

The Penalty for Procrastination

This table shows you how much your monthly payment must be, earning 10% a year, to reach a million dollars by age 65. The longer you wait to get started, the higher the monthly payment must be in order to achieve the goal.

Starting Age	Monthly Payment	Annual Payments	Total Out-of-Pocket
20	$95.40	$1,145	$51,516
25	$158.13	$1,898	$75,902
30	$263.39	$3,161	$110,624
35	$442.38	$5,309	$159,257
40	$753.67	$9,044	$226,101
45	$1,316.88	$15,803	$316,051
50	$2,412.72	$28,953	$434,290
55	$4,881.74	$58,581	$585,809

Taxes Are Your Enemy

If we assume that a 28% income tax bracket effectively reduces a 10% rate of return to a 7.2% rate of return, this table shows you the impact this has on your ending values, for a monthly investment of $264.

# of Years	Earning 10% a Year	Earning 7.2% a Year		Difference
10	54,079	46,201		7,878
15	109,420	85,148		24,272
20	200,473	140,913		59,560
25	350,284	220,757		129,527
30	596,769	335,076		261,693
35	1,002,312	498,756		503,556
	1,002,312	498,756		
less 28% taxes:	-280,647	N/A		
	721,665 -	498,756	=	222,909

BEWARE OF THE MONEY MONSTER

There's one last unpleasant fact of life we need to discuss because it affects each and every one of us - whether we're striving to become millionaires or not. That's inflation. It's a money monster because it gobbles up money - your money.

It's dangerous because it's very subtle. You don't even realize your money is being gobbled up by this monster because it only eats a little at a time. The problem is, it eats constantly. Over time, if you do not take preventive measures, it will literally eat you "out of house and home."

Here's how it works. Every year, generally speaking, things cost a little more than they did the year before. Not much more, and not all things rise in price in unison or at a uniform rate. Some years, some things cost a lot more, some things cost only a little more. Some things may even cost less, before they eventually cost more. If things cost less than they did the year before, it's called deflation (an abnormal and temporary state of affairs). When things cost more it's called inflation.

Over the last 70 years or so, since the government started tracking such things, we're told that inflation has averaged between 3% and 4% a year. Let's use 4% for the sake of our discussion from this point forward.

If a loaf of bread cost $1.00 this year, at 4% inflation it will cost $1.04 next year. A $10,000 car will cost $10,400 the next year, and a $150,000 house will cost $156,000. In ten years that same loaf of bread will cost $1.48, the car $14,800, and the home $231,000. In twenty years, the loaf of bread will cost $2.19, the car $21,900, and the home $342,000.

Little by little, bite by bite, that 4% a year really adds up. After ten years things cost 48% more. After twenty years they will have more than doubled, costing 119% more. **After twenty years it takes more than twice as much money to buy the same goods and services.**

Looking at it another way, the purchasing power of your dollar is eroding. What you get for a $1.00 this year will only deliver 96 cents' worth next year, and only 93 cents the year after that. In ten years that same dollar only buys two thirds of what it did when you started. **In twenty years, that same dollar buys less than half of what it did at the start.**

Just a little bite, hardly noticeable one year at a time. Over time the money monster can hurt you very badly. It's the miracle of compounding, only working against you, like taxes. Over time your dollars will only buy a fraction of what they buy today. **Over ten years, your purchasing power is cut by a third. Over twenty years, your purchasing power is cut in half.**

WHERE'S THE MONEY GOING TO COME FROM?

Maybe your salary has also been rising 4% a year, but maybe it hasn't. If it does, you can keep pace and stay even (but who wants to stay even all of their life - wouldn't you want to get ahead?). You can almost learn to live with the money monster if it's not killing you. As long as your salary has been rising along with the prices of everything you have to buy with your salary, you will keep the money monster at bay.

What happens when you stop working? Your salary stops. But your living needs certainly don't. And the prices you'll pay to meet your needs continue to rise whether you pay for them from a salary or otherwise. Most people want to retire from working at their regular jobs at some point in their lives. Many people simply are unable to work at their former occupations past a certain age. Whether you stop working by choice or by physical necessity, you've still got the rest of your life ahead of you! Living costs money! Over twenty years it takes twice as much money. Where will the money come from?

The government estimates the majority of the money will come from you. Social Security will provide less than a third of what you'll need (if you're lucky). Corporate pension plans may provide about a third (if you even have one, and worked long enough at the same place to be entitled to it). The balance must come from you and your lifetime of savings and investments. Your long-term quality of life is dependent upon the choices you make today. Time will either work for you or against you. Taxes work against you, as does inflation.

There seems to be no way of killing the money monster. It's like a virus for which man has been unable to find a cure for the thousands of years money itself has been in existence. But the monster can be tamed. Even though it cannot be defeated, it can be controlled. Like death and taxes, we've learned to live with inflation.

Inflation the Money Monster takes just a little bite, hardly noticeable, one year at a time. Over time, however, the money monster can hurt you very badly.

It's the miracle of compounding, only working against you, like taxes. Over time your dollars will only buy a fraction of what they buy today.

Over ten years, your purchasing power is cut by a third.

Over twenty years, your purchasing power is cut in half.

HOW TO LIVE ON A MILLION DOLLARS, MORE, OR LESS

What does Financial Independence mean to you? To many people it means never having to work for money again. There's a difference between *having* to work for money and choosing to work for money, but when you are financially independent the decision is 100% yours to make. Isn't this why you want to become a millionaire?

Financial Independence means you've accumulated enough money sufficient to meet all of your financial needs for the rest of your life.

Financial Independence means your accumulated capital - your nest egg - is large enough to meet all of your income needs for the rest of your life. Financial Independence means you will never run out of money no matter how long you live.

How much money does it take to get to this point?

The actual amount will differ from one person to the next, but the process to calculate it is the same for everybody. This process is described in detail in the next chapter.

What does Financial Independence mean to you? To many people it means never having to work for money again.

Financial Independence means you've accumulated enough money sufficient to meet all of your financial needs for the rest of your life.

THE POINT-ZERO-SIX SOLUTION

Ask yourself how much money you would like to receive every year, year in and out, to completely support yourself. Then take this number and divide it by Point-Zero-Six, and you will have your answer.

Why Point-Zero-Six? Well, it starts with the assumption that you can grow your nest egg at an average annual rate of 10% a year, and continues with the assumption that inflation will remain below its historical average annual rate of 4%. Given these assumptions, you would be able to withdraw 6% of your capital every year and never run out of money. At the end of each year all you do is take the ending value of your portfolio, withdraw 6% of it, and live off of the 6% for the next year.

As long as the assumptions hold true, with 6% withdrawals your capital will never be depleted, your nest egg will support you with an annual income for the rest of your life, and you will always keep pace with inflation, meaning the purchasing power of your dollar will never erode no matter how long you live.

Some years you may be able to earn substantially more than 10% on your investments, some years you may earn substantially less. In some years your investments will likely even decline in value. Inflation must also comply by remaining below its historical 3% to 4% average annual rate of the last seventy-plus years. So there are no guarantees, but assuming you can grow your money at an average of 10%, and inflation behaves, withdrawing 6% of your nest egg each year would enable you to support yourself, with no erosion of purchasing power, for the rest of your life no matter how long you live.

Taking out 6% a year is how we get to Point-Zero-Six (.06) as the divisor. In other words, if you want $40,000 a year in annual income, all of it coming from your own hard-earned capital, you divide $40,000 by Point-Zero-Six and you get $667,000 as the size of your required nest egg. 6% of $667,000 gets you $40,000 every year. If you want $50,000 a year, you'll need $833,333. If you want $60,000 a year, you'll need $1,000,000.

If you achieve your goal of becoming a millionaire, and if the assumptions hold true, and you employ the 6% withdrawal system, you will receive $60,000 a year in income - for the rest of your life.

Can you survive on $60,000 a year? That's $5,000 a month. Can you live on $5,000 a month? This is your "pension" from a benevolent employer: you and your money. It's one of the perks of being a member of The Millionaires Club! Do you know anyone who's receiving a lifetime pension of $5,000 a month?

Even better, once you die, your millionaire "pension" continues to be paid out to your heirs, and to *their* heirs, and to *their* heirs, forever and forever. There isn't a corporate pension plan in the world that will do this.

The eventual size of your nest egg will determine whether you live on a million dollars, more than a million dollars, or less than a million dollars. The decisions you make today and tomorrow will determine the eventual size of your nest egg and the annual income it can generate for you.

Are you willing to sacrifice $264 a month today (and stick with it for 35 years), in exchange for $5,000 a month later (which you and your loved ones will receive for the rest of your lives)?

Even if you don't have any great desire to leave a legacy that lasts for generations, don't you want the absolute best for yourself and the people who are most important to you in your life?

Your Desired Annual Income,
divided by point-zero-six, equals
Your Required Nest Egg.

$60,000 divided by .06 equals $1,000,000

Can you live on $60,000 a year for the rest of your life?

The decisions you make today and tomorrow will determine the eventual size of your nest egg and the annual income it can generate for you.

Part Three

THE MECHANICS OF BECOMING A MILLIONAIRE

THE FIRST GOLDEN RULE FOR BECOMING A MILLIONAIRE

The First Golden Rule is this: Spend less than you Earn.

There are really only two things you can do with the money you earn. You can SPEND it or SAVE it.

In order to become a millionaire you must choose SAVE over SPEND for some percentage of your money.

The *larger* the percentage of your money you choose to SAVE instead of SPEND, the quicker you will achieve your Millionaire goal.

Let's face it. Most of the money that comes your way is already marked SPEND. You must make a conscious decision to erase SPEND on some of your money and mark it SAVE instead. You must choose to convert some of your dollars from SPEND to SAVE. It requires a change in how you think about your money. It also requires a practical change in your life style, because it means you will have to do without something you would acquire through spending. You will have to NOT-SPEND in order to SAVE. This isn't always easy to do. You must, however, do it. I think you know this.

Let me help you change your money philosophy.

A part of all you earn is yours to KEEP. KEEP is another word for SAVE. Another way to look at SAVING is ACCUMULATING CAPITAL. The capital you manage to accumulate will eventually support you financially. Every SPEND dollar you manage to convert into a SAVE dollar will be put to work for you earning more money.

You only have to convert that earned dollar into capital once. You yourself will never have to work for that original SAVE dollar again! Your SAVE dollar begins working for YOU! It starts working for you immediately, and it continues working for you *forever*.

As the SAVE dollar earns more money for you, it grows and grows. Thanks to the Miracle of Compounding, it's possible to have that original SAVE dollar grow into two dollars, and then four dollars, and on and on. Eventually it is possible for the capital you accumulate to earn enough money to support you financially for the rest of your life. In other words, instead of you having to work at a job to earn money, you have enough of your money working for you so that you no longer need a job.

When your capital grows to an accumulated $1,000,000, you become a millionaire. Recall our millionaire mathematics: depending on how much you save and when you start, it's possible you only have to save $111,000 or 11% of your million dollars. The other 89%, or $889,000 comes from the growth of your savings!

The question to ask yourself is: how quickly do you want to become a millionaire? Your answer determines your SAVE and SPEND decisions from this day forward.

A part of all you earn is yours to keep. In order to become a millionaire you must continually SAVE some of the money you earn.

The First Golden Rule for Becoming a Millionaire is this: Spend less than you Earn.

A part of all you earn is yours to keep. Every dollar you SAVE is one more dollar you put to work for you, and is one more dollar you will never have to work for again.

The more you choose to SAVE instead of Spend, the quicker you will become a Millionaire.

THE SECOND GOLDEN RULE FOR BECOMING A MILLIONAIRE

The Second Golden Rule is this: Invest the Difference (between what you earn and what you spend) in Appreciating Assets.

Appreciating means increasing in value. Assets are things that you own. You want to own things that increase in value because it is the best way to grow your savings.

There are two ways to generate the income you need in which to live: you can work for it yourself or you can generate it from the assets you own. The assets themselves may produce income, or you can produce the income you need by selling off a piece of your assets as you need the income. If you accumulate enough appreciating assets you will always have pieces to sell without ever running out. The longer you hold your appreciating assets, the more valuable they become. As time goes on, you expect to be able to get more and more money for the pieces you sell.

Assets usually take time to increase in value. Typically the longer the time the more valuable they become. Assets also fluctuate in value. Sometimes they go up in value a little, sometimes they go up in value a lot. Sometimes they go down in value. Depending upon when you buy them and when you sell them, they could be worth more or less than what you paid when you bought them. It all depends upon the market for those assets at the time of your transaction. The idea is that in the long-term appreciating assets will be worth more than they were at an earlier point in time, despite the short-term fluctuations in value.

You can own things which go down in value over time, which are called *depreciating* assets. They include things like cars, computers, furniture, appliances, clothes, etc. You pay one price to own them and you receive less than you paid should you try to sell them. They become worth less and less as time goes on.

Appreciating assets, in contrast, are assets which have historically increased in value, especially over long periods of time. They include: common stocks, real estate, and some collectibles like art, coins, stamps, antiques, etc. Common stocks represent ownership interests in businesses, and they increase in value as the underlying businesses grow more valuable. Real estate may include your own home and/or property you rent out to others, and it increases in value when more and more people desire ownership of it. Collectibles increase in value under the same principle: because they are relatively rare and their supply is limited, the more people desire ownership the more they are willing to pay, and the more valuable they become.

Buying such assets is called Investing, which is defined as "committing money in order to earn a financial return" and "to make use of for future benefits." When you invest the difference between what you earn and what you spend, which is your savings, you commit this money in order to earn a financial return to make use of for future benefits.

Committing the money means you have to do without it. You have to leave it alone and give it the time it needs to grow in value. The longer the time you commit the money the longer the assets have to grow in value and the greater the financial return to you. The financial return you are seeking is that your investments grow in value over time and are worth far more than what you paid when you acquired them. The future benefit of this is that you become a Millionaire and live off your assets for the rest of your life.

A part of all you earn is yours to keep, and you are investing this part for the future benefit of becoming a Millionaire. To achieve this goal you need to invest your savings in appreciating assets. You need to commit your savings to buying ownership interests in assets which you expect to grow in value over time, and holding those assets for as long as it takes to become a Millionaire.

This book will teach you how to find and invest in assets which have historically appreciated in value. This is how others have become Millionaires, and it is how you too can become a Millionaire.

The Second Golden Rule for Becoming A Millionaire is this: Invest the Difference between what you Earn and what you Spend in Appreciating Assets.

You must commit your savings to buying ownership interests in assets which you expect to increase in value over time, and holding those assets for as long as it takes to become a Millionaire.

This is how others have become Millionaires, and it is how you too can become a Millionaire.

THE SECRET FORMULA FOR BECOMING A MILLIONAIRE

You just learned that the First Golden Rule for Becoming a Millionaire is SPEND less than you EARN. The Secret Formula is the mathematical expression of the first Golden Rule.

The difference between what you EARN and what you SPEND is what you SAVE. The average person sees the formula just this way:

EARN - SPEND = SAVE

Most people pay their bills and spend their money and try to save whatever is ever left over. Yet those same people wonder why there's so much month left over at the end of their money. They've run out of spending money before the end of the month, which of course also means that not a dollar went into savings.

You, however, are not the average person. You are an aspiring millionaire! By the very fact that you have found your way to this book, and to this page, proves you are not the average person.

The ones who ultimately succeed in becoming millionaires understand that the key to success is looking at the conventional formula just a little differently. But this little difference makes all the difference in the world. It can determine whether or not you'll become a millionaire.

The secret formula for becoming a millionaire:

EARN - SAVE = SPEND

In this formula, saving comes first. Spending takes the back seat, where it belongs. You get to SPEND whatever is left over *after* you SAVE.

It doesn't matter how much or how little you earn, it's what you do with your money that counts. If prosperity is more important to you than poverty, then saving must take precedence over spending. A part of all you earn is yours to keep, forever. Your savings must come right off the top. The remainder is yours to spend any way you want.

Millionaires are savers. Do your math. The numbers work as perfectly and as timelessly as the planets orbit around the sun. If you save enough money you *will* become a millionaire.

HOW TO PUT THE SECRET FORMULA FOR BECOMING A MILLIONAIRE TO MAXIMUM ADVANTAGE FOR YOU

Use a double-pronged approach. Work on both the SAVE part and on the EARN part.

Start with SAVE. The quickest and easiest way to find money to save, and to increase the amount you are able to save, is to simply spend less. Spending less takes the pressure off of feeling like there isn't enough to do both - save and pay bills.

Virtually everyone can take a close look at their financial life and see where some of their money is slipping through the cracks because they are not being as careful with their money as they could be. Look at where your money is going. What are you spending money on that might be obtained for less than you are currently paying? What are you wasting money on?

There are hundreds of ways to save money. Entire books have been written on how to save money by spending less. See the *Bibliography* at the end of this book for a couple of titles.

The second prong of the strategy is to look at the EARN side of the equation. Think of ways you can increase the amount of money you bring into your life. Perhaps you have a talent or hobby you can turn into a regular money-generating system.

Maybe you've got things to sell to generate cash. Are you hanging on to things that do not serve you anymore? Others may find value in these things even if you no longer do. Convert these items into cash and put the cash to work for you.

How is your career progressing? Perhaps your next promotion and raise are yours for the asking. Perhaps you're considering a job change. A salary increase often accompanies such changes. Again, see the *Bibliography* for more books that can help you.

Whether it's spending less or earning more, remember the secret formula for becoming a Millionaire and apply it to your life, starting today.

If prosperity is more important to you than poverty, then saving must take precedence over spending. A part of all you earn is yours to keep, forever. Your savings must come right off the top. The remainder is yours to spend any way you want.

If you save enough money you *will* become a Millionaire.

LOAN AND OWN

Just as there are only two things you can do with the money you earn - spend it or save it - there are only two things you can do with your savings. You can loan them out, or you can use them to buy an investment outright whereby you become an owner (or part-owner) of that investment. Both methods can be used to grow your money.

The Second Golden Rule for Becoming a Millionaire is to use your savings to own assets that appreciate in value. This is the best method to grow your money over the long run. As you prepare to grow your money it is important you learn why this is so, and it begins with a discussion on the difference between being a Loaner and an Owner.

When you loan your money, you can expect to receive interest from the borrower in return for the temporary use of your money. You know in advance how much interest you can expect to receive over the course of the loan, and you know in advance when you can expect your money to be returned to you. When the loan ends it is said to have matured, and the maturity date is the date you expect your money to be returned to you.

When you choose to own something instead, you use your money to buy an ownership interest in something. When making this type of investment, your money is not returned to you. Instead, you hope that the ownership interest you're taking will become more valuable over time. You hope to someday be able to sell your ownership position for more than you paid for it, and earn yourself a profit.

All investments can be classified into either of these two categories. They are either Loanership or Ownership investments.

LOANERSHIP INVESTMENTS

When you deposit your money at the bank you are making a loanership investment. The bank is actually borrowing your money to use in the course of its business. It uses your money to make loans to other people. The bank pays you interest for the privilege of using your money, in the same way the bank's loan customers pay it interest for the privilege of using the "bank's" money. The bank makes money by charging a higher interest rate on the loans it makes compared to the interest it pays people for keeping their money in the bank.

You can receive your money "on demand" simply by withdrawing it (by writing a check if it's a checking account). The bank is obligated by law to return your money on demand. You may agree to leave your money in the bank for a certain length of time in exchange for a higher rate of interest. These are called Certificates of Deposit (CDs), and you can usually find them in maturities ranging from three months all the way up to five years. The more money you agree to tie up in any given CD, the higher the interest rate the bank is willing to pay. A $10,000 1-year CD should pay more than a $1,000 1-year CD. Also, the longer the time frame you agree to tie up your money, the higher the interest rate the bank is willing to pay. A 5-year CD should pay substantially more than a 90-day CD.

The United States Government has a seemingly insatiable need to borrow money, and it issues debt securities in exchange for the money people lend to it. You can get U.S. Treasury Bills (T-Bills) which mature in 3 months, 6 months, or a year. You can get Treasury Notes which mature in 1 to 10 ten years. And you can get U.S. Treasury Bonds which mature in more than 10 years (typically 30 years). State and local governments issue municipal bonds in order to borrow money. Corporations issue corporate bonds to borrow money. Bonds are typically issued with maturities of 30 years.

All of these are loanership investments. Whether the borrower is your friend, your bank, the United States Government, the State of California, the City of New York, or Coca-Cola, you are making a loan. The borrower promises to pay you interest in exchange for using your money, and the borrower promises to return your money (the principal) at a pre-determined date in the future.

Some municipal governments and corporations have better credit ratings than others, due to their greater financial stability, longer operating histories, and established credit performance. The more likely an entity will meet its obligations of paying the interest it promises to pay, and returning the principal at maturity as promised, the lower the interest it has to pay on the money it borrows. The greater the risk the borrower might default on either of its promises, the greater the interest it must promise pay to attract the money it wants to borrow.

Sometimes people lend their money by buying a bond and later decide they are unable or unwilling to wait until maturity to get their money back. A whole marketplace exists for the buying and selling of bonds. You can sell your bond to someone else who steps into your shoes as the new lender. The borrower is notified of the change and pays the interest to the new bondholder. The bond may change hands many times over the course of its life. Whoever holds the bond at maturity is the one who gets the original principal, at full value, returned by the borrower.

Should you decide to sell before maturity, you may get more or less than you originally paid for the bond, regardless of whether you were the original lender. The price you receive is determined by what interest rates are at the time you sell. If your bond is paying 6% a year in interest, which was the rate when you bought it, but interest rates on new bonds being issued today are paying 8%, nobody will pay you full price for your lower-paying bond. They'll pay you something for it, but it'll be less than you paid for it. Conversely, if interest rates today are down to 4% on similar bonds, people will gladly pay you more than you paid for your higher-paying bond because it's better than what can be had today.

OWNERSHIP INVESTMENTS

When you take an ownership interest you exchange your money for an equity position. You are buying the investment to own it. When you buy a house you make a down payment and borrow money to finance the rest of the purchase. Each monthly payment pays down the loan and increases your equity position in the home. Eventually you pay off the loan and own the home free and clear. You may buy real estate for investment purposes and do the same thing.

You may start your own business, or buy an existing business to operate. You may buy part or all of an existing business and leave the managing of that business to someone else. If that business is a "publicly-held" business, you buy shares of stock in that business and become part-owner along with thousands of other people.

In all of these examples, you are exchanging your money for an ownership position with the hope and expectation that your ownership interest grows in value over time. You do not receive interest income, nor do you receive your money back at any given point in the future, because this transaction is not a loan. (Some businesses regularly share part of their earnings with their shareholders in the form of dividends which, although it's not interest income from a loan, is income just the same). The only way to get your original money out of the transaction is to sell your ownership interest. You receive no guarantee or formal assurance of any kind that your ownership interest will become more valuable over time. So when you do sell, it may be for more or less than your original cost.

There are different risks involved with both loanership and ownership investments. Let's take a closer look at these risks.

All investments can be classified as either a Loanership or Ownership investment.

You can either loan your savings out and collect interest in return, or you can exchange your money for an ownership position in something, with the hope and expectation that your ownership position grows in value over time.

RISK

When investors talk about risk, they usually mean the possibility that they will lose some or all of their money. This is an excellent definition of risk! Although it is an excellent definition of risk, it is a terrible reason for not investing. Yet many people use it as a convenient excuse for not taking the time to educate themselves on how to manage risk to achieve worthwhile and rewarding financial results. Some people are just not interested, others too busy, or too lazy. Whatever the reason, the end result is tragic. None of these people will become millionaires.

Knowledge is power. First we learn how and why we can lose money in our investments by identifying the risks we take. Then we learn what we can do to manage those risks as best we can in order to reduce their influence in our efforts to achieve our goal of becoming a millionaire.

You may be chagrined to learn that there are actually a number of different ways of losing value in an investment! This is really just another way of saying that there are a number of different risks, each of which affect investment values in different ways, for different reasons. In order to manage risk as a whole, we need to be able to identify the individual risks. That's exactly what we will do now.

Market risk refers to the possibility of losing value on your particular investments due to the fact that the *market* for those particular investments declines as a whole. It is the opposite effect of "a rising tide raises all boats". An ebbing tide lowers all boats. In any market there are buyers and sellers, and at any given time the balance may shift in either direction, for all kinds of reasons. A market rises when more people are interested in buying than in selling, and it declines when more people wish to sell than to buy.

It's not just your investment, it's the whole market for those investments which includes yours.

Business risk refers to the possibility of losing value on your particular investment, regardless of what is happening in the market as a whole, due to the individual business underlying that investment. Circumstances pertaining to the specific company in which you are invested may have changed for the negative, which negatively impact your investment in that company. The fundamental value of a specific investment is directly dependent upon a company's ability to generate sales and earnings, and maintain financial stability and predictability. Should investors decide, right or wrong, that these are threatened in some way, there will be more sellers than buyers in that particular investment and the values drop accordingly.

Default risk refers to the possibility of losing value in a particular investment because the specific company in which you've invested fails to meet its promises and obligations to its creditors. It may fail to make interest payments in full and/or on time, and it may fail to repay borrowed principal in full and/or on time. This is the same kind of risk a bank takes on when it makes loans to people. In the investment world, it is the people making the loans to governments and corporations, and they assume default risk as an inherent part of the transaction.

Liquidity risk refers to the possibility that an investor will not be able to sell an investment as quickly as desired (or, conversely, to buy an investment as quickly as desired to take advantage of a perceived opportunity), and the delay results in a loss of value of that investment.

Interest Rate risk refers to the possibility of losing value in a particular investment due to changes in interest rates in the economy as a whole. Interest rates fluctuate, depending upon what the economy as a whole is doing. The interest rate paid by a specific investment in relation to the interest rates currently available in the economy will affect the value of that specific investment.

The main thing to remember about interest rates is that they have an inverse relationship with loanership investment values. When interest rates rise, bonds fall in value. When interest rates fall, bond values rise. The longer the time to the maturity of a bond, the greater the sensitivity to interest rate changes (a long-term-bond will experience a greater change in value than a short-term bond). Refer to the last paragraph of *Loanership Investments* in the previous chapter for a refresher.

Call risk pertains to loanership investments and refers to the possibility that your invested money will be returned to you sooner than you expected and sooner than you desired. Many bond issuers (borrowers) reserve the right to pay off their debt and "call" in bonds before they mature. They usually do this to take advantage of interest rate declines. If interest rates fall since the original issuing of the bonds, they can pay off the old loan and get a new one at lower interest rates, saving them lots of money. When they exercise this right it means you (as the lender/investor) will lose the income stream you were getting from the investment. Once your invested principal is returned to you, you are faced with reinvesting it, at potentially lower interest rates and a reduced income stream to you. This is Reinvestment risk.

Reinvestment risk refers to the possibility that interest rates will have come down when it comes time to reinvest some money which was previously-invested at higher interest rates. If your loanership investment was earning 8%, and it matures or you sell it or the borrower pays you off early, and current interest rates for similar investments are only earning 6%, you will earn less than you did on the original investment.

Inflation risk is the possibility that price increases will spiral out of control, which causes the purchasing power of the dollar to lose value. Recall our earlier discussion on Inflation the Money Monster and the havoc it reaps on your money over time.

Tax Rate risk refers to the possibility that the government changes tax rates which negatively impact currently-held investments.

Economic risk refers to the possibility that the economy will falter, which occurs when interest rates rise, unemployment increases, and budget and trade deficits increase. These macroeconomic influences cause business productivity, sales, and earnings to suffer which in turn causes the market prices of investments to decline.

Political risk mostly refers to the possibility of political instability in the governments of foreign countries, which may change those countries' policies with regard to foreign investors, adversely affecting the value of investments in those countries.

Currency risk refers to the possibility that the valuations of any country's currency may lose value and have a detrimental effect on the sales and earnings of companies transacting business in that currency, which causes investments in those companies to also lose value.

Principal risk (also known as Capital risk) refers to the possibility that an investment drops in value, regardless of the reason. Price volatility underscores this risk. Prices of investments never stay they same. As investments are subjected to the above risks, they are priced accordingly. Prices go up and down, and Principal risk refers to the possibility of prices going down.

RISK and FEAR

This brings us full circle, for Principal risk is the real issue. All of the other individual risks we just described are the many ways investments may lose value. All of them put principal at risk. When people say they don't want to invest it is because they are afraid they will lose money.

It all boils down to fear. Fear stops people dead in their tracks, paralyzing them from further action or any action at all. It's perfectly normal and acceptable to feel fear, but you can't let it stop you. Not in investing, and not in life as a whole.

The solution is to understand your risks, and manage them as best you can in order to minimize their impact. You will learn how to manage risk in a subsequent chapter. You will note that every time Risk and Return are discussed together anywhere, Risk appears first in the discussion. That's because Risk appears first in real life. Your Rewards are directly related the Risk you are willing to assume. You'll never find a millionaire who didn't assume the necessary risk. You too must assume risk in order to become a millionaire. You won't become a millionaire if you allow fear to dominate your investment life. You're going to need to feel the fear and do it anyway. If you don't, you'll be assuming the greatest risk of all.

You'll never find a millionaire who didn't assume the necessary risk. You too must assume risk in order to become a millionaire.

THE GREATEST RISK OF ALL

The greatest risk of all is what I call Wealth Risk.

Wealth Risk refers to the possibility that the wealth you accumulate over the course of your life will be insufficient to meet your needs later in life when you are no longer able to work to generate the income you need to survive financially.

This will come as no surprise to you but it's important to remind you that the body and mind at age 70 are not the same body and mind at age 20. Neither is the job marketplace the same for 70-year-olds as it is for 20-year-olds.

Your greatest fear should be the possibility of outliving your income. We all know people living on "fixed incomes" who are no longer able to work and whose fixed incomes are eroded year after year by inflation. The cost of living rises faster than the fixed incomes. Over time it results in poverty.

Social Security was never intended to be the full and total financial support for the retired worker. Corporate pensions, unlike previous generations, are no longer adequate in completely meeting the retired worker's needs. These resources may help you, if they are available to you when the time comes, but greatest part of your income later in life will need to come from the amount of wealth you accumulate over the course of your life.

We are living longer than ever before in the history of the human race. The average life expectancy in the United States has been rising steadily and now stands at 71-plus years. "Average" means that a lot of people don't make it to age 71, and lots of people live to ages far beyond age 71.

People are spending twenty five years and more in retirement. It could be one-fourth to one-third of your life! "Retirement" means they are no longer working at full-time careers. "Spending" means they are still spending money. In twenty-five years prices can rise four-fold or more. The cost of living can be four times higher than it was twenty-five years earlier. The same dollar might buy a fourth of what it once did, so it takes four dollars to just stay even with that same dollar twenty-five years ago. Return again and again to this chapter and to the Money Monster-Inflation chapter.

Your quality of life in the later years of your life is directly dependent upon your savings and investments program over the course of your life.

Nobody ultimately chooses to live in poverty, but that's the end result of the choices they made over the course of their lives. Failing to make a choice is still a choice. Failure to accept investment risk, and the responsibility for managing investment risk, does not leave you without risk. By default you're accepting and assuming Wealth Risk, and this is the greatest risk of all!

Failure to accept investment risk, and the responsibility for managing investment risk, does not leave you without risk. By default you're accepting and assuming Wealth Risk, and this is the greatest risk of all!

HOW TO MANAGE RISK

Let's take a look at each of the Risks in the *Risk* chapter, and let's pretend that we are *forced* to assume each one! We'll pretend we have absolutely no choice in the matter. Since there is no way to avoid these risks, we'll do the next best thing and examine how we might manage each risk to our best advantage. Thumb back to the *Risk* chapter for a refresher on any of these risks.

Market risk Being invested in more than one market reduces your dependency on any single market. US markets are different from European, Asian-Pacific, and Latin American markets. Likewise, the stock market, bond market, and real estate market are all different markets within the same country, and each of these markets responds differently to the factors which influence them.

Business risk Investing in a single business puts all of your eggs in a single basket, and all of your capital rides on the success or failure of that business. Think of investing as a window. A single investment is one large window pane. If a ball crashes through that single pane, your entire window is destroyed. If you have investments in many businesses, your window has many different panes of glass, each separated and protected from the others by its own window frame. If a ball crashes through the window, it only destroys a small pane or two, leaving the majority of the remaining panes intact.

Default risk Again, investing in more than one entity reduces the impact and your overall risk should any single one of them default on its obligations. Also, different classes of borrowers have different likelihoods of defaulting. The U.S. Government is less likely to default on its obligations than a corporation. Among corporations, one which has a history of eighty years of proven positive credit history behind it is less likely to default on its obligations than one which has only been around five years. Different countries around the world have different credit ratings too. Spreading your capital out to different classes of borrowers further reduces your dependency on the performance of any one of them.

Liquidity risk You want to keep your money working for you at all times, yet you need to be able to get to some cash immediately should you need it. You may even have to sell investments on short notice, so you want to be sure you can find a buyer quickly. The solution is to be partially invested in markets with ready buyers and sellers: the stock market which is more liquid than the real estate market.

Additionally you hope that at the time of the sale you can get at least as much out of the investment as you put into it (not sell at a loss). The solution here is to always have some of your money invested in places where the principal is expected to remain relatively stable over time in comparison to other investments.

Interest Rate risk If you have loanership investments which mature at different points in time, you can protect yourself from adverse changes in rates and even position yourself to benefit from these changes. If interest rates are declining, the long-term investments you made earlier are locked in at the earlier higher rates. But the short-term investments you make will be going in at the newer lower rates. If interest rates are rising, your long-term rates are locked at those earlier lower rates, but your short term investments can go in at the newer higher rates. Mid-range, intermediate-term investments provide a nice balance between the short-term and long-term. So have short-term, intermediate-term, and long-term loanership investments instead of having all of your loanership money coming back to you at the same time.

Also, different investments react differently to changes in interest rates. Long-term loanership investments are generally more sensitive than short-term loanership investments. Ownership investments like stocks are affected differently than loanership investments like bonds. And real estate, another ownership investment, is affected differently than stocks. Spreading out your investments reduces your dependency (and risk) on any one type of investment, and actually helps position you to possibly benefit in some way regardless of what interest rates are doing.

Call risk Again, don't put all your eggs in one basket when you know in advance the basketholder has the right to return your eggs at his discretion. He'll return your eggs when they're better off staying and growing in the basket.

Reinvestment risk The same discussion on Interest Rate risk applies here.

Inflation risk The way to manage inflation risk is to invest in areas that will grow your money faster than inflation is growing. The greater the distance you can put between the rate of the growth of your investments and the rate of inflation, the better off you will be. The longer the time you stay ahead of inflation, the better off you are. Of the two classes, ownership investments do a far superior job of outpacing inflation in comparison to loanership investments. (But you should not put all of your money entirely into ownership investments, as we shall discuss later).

Tax rate risk It has often been said that the only two guarantees we have in life are death and taxes. Our politicians are endlessly modifying our tax laws, whether creating new taxes to impose or endlessly modifying the rules on existing taxes. The best way to manage your risk in this area is by learning all about the ways these tax laws affect you and your money, and then taking the fullest advantage of the laws in order to protect and grow your money. This is what large corporations and wealthy individuals do, and this is what you should do too.

Economic risk It is a fact of life that business cycles move from expansion and growth to contraction and recession, then back again. What cannot be predicted is the magnitude and length of any one stage of the cycle. The markets do however anticipate the changes, and investment values are influenced accordingly. Different industries (and their underlying businesses and investments in those businesses) are influenced differently by the various stages of the business cycle. (Some investments actually do well when times are bad). One way to manage economic risk is to be invested across an array of different industries. Another way is to be invested in different economies throughout the world. Even though all business cycles go through the same stages, they don't all go through them the same way at the same time.

Political risk and Currency risk Again, investing around the world reduces some of your exposure to these two risks when your investment capital is not dependent upon any single country. You will learn more about worldwide investing in a later chapter.

Principal risk By now you may have realized a few things about risk. Although each of the individual risks affects your principal, and many of the risks are associated with each other, they do not all affect your principal in the same way, for the same reasons, at the same time. The conclusion you should reach is that *the best way to manage Principal risk is to spread out your exposure to the many individual risks.* This is known in the investment world as Diversification, and we have much more to say about this, so stay tuned.

Wealth risk The best way to manage Wealth risk is to follow the Golden Rules: Spend less than you Earn and Pay Yourself First. Put your Greatest Ally in the World - Time - to work for you. Challenge your two Greatest Enemies in the World - Procrastination and Taxes - with every tool you have available to you. Protect your money from the Money Monster - Inflation - by investing your savings in vehicles which outpace inflation in order to grow your money faster than inflation eats it up. Assume the Risk necessary to reap the Reward necessary to build your wealth over time, but manage those risks carefully.

Assume the Risk necessary to reap the Reward necessary to build your wealth over time, but manage those risks carefully.

RISK AND REWARD

In investing, as in life, you are rewarded for taking on risk. Everybody knows this as the Risk-Return Trade-Off, but you should take time to truly understand what this means.

It might help you to think of "Return" as your Reward for investing. ***Your investing reward is directly related to the amount of risk you're willing to assume.*** The more risk you take on, the greater your reward. The lower the risk, the lower the reward. You trade off risk for reward.

Loanership investments like savings accounts, money market accounts, Certificates of Deposit, U.S. Treasury Bills, government and corporate bonds are better at protecting you from *Principal* risk because values tend to fluctuate less than they do with Ownership investments. This is especially true in the short-term. The prices of Loanership investments are subject to less volatility than the prices of Ownership investments.

In the long run, however, Ownership investments like stocks and real estate tend to far outperform Loanership investments in terms of protecting you from *Wealth* risk because Ownership investments do a much better job of growing your money over time. The price you pay for the short-term stability offered by Loanership investments ultimately puts your principal at risk because Inflation the Money Monster erodes the purchasing power of your principal. Ownership investments protect you from the Money Monster better than Loanership investments.

If it's stability of principal you're after, Loanership investments are for you. If it's growth of principal you're after, Ownership investments are for you. There is a place in your life for both types of investments. However, **if you want to become a millionaire, growth of principal will be your major objective**

and you will need to rely predominantly on Ownership investments.

Another way to look at the risk-reward tradeoff: ***if you don't want the risk, don't expect the reward!***

The people who are willing to take on risk should be rewarded for taking on that risk. The ones who aren't willing to assume the risk should not be rewarded.

Investing is just like life, isn't it? It really is all about going for the rewards, and having the guts to do it. What holds us back? Fear! What reduces fear? Knowledge! Knowledge is power. Let's expand upon your knowledge about Risk and the Rewards for accepting Risk in the investment world.

Your investing reward is directly related to the amount of risk you're willing to assume. The more risk you take on, the greater your reward. The lower the risk, the lower the reward. You trade off risk for reward.

If you want to become a millionaire, growth of principal will be your major objective and you will need to rely predominantly on ownership investments.

REWARD

Here are the average annual returns over the course of the 72 years from 1926 through 1997, for the following types of investments here in the United States, before accounting for inflation (the average annual rate for which is also presented).

Small Company Stocks	12.7%
Large Company Stocks	11.0%
Long-Term Government Bonds	5.3%
U.S. Treasury Bills	3.8%
Inflation	3.1%

(Source: Ibbotson Associates, Chicago, IL).

WHAT YOU NEED TO KNOW ABOUT THIS DATA

The return for Smaller Company Stocks is derived from the Ibbotson Small Company Index. The prices of small company stocks generally are more volatile than the prices of large company stocks. The return for Large Company Stocks is derived from the Standard & Poor's Composite Index of 500 Stocks (S&P500), which is a group of unmanaged securities widely regarded by investors to be representative of large-company stocks in general. The results shown assume the reinvestment of dividends. An investment cannot be made directly into an index. The Long Term

Government Bonds used in this illustration have a maturity of approximately 20 years. U.S. Treasury Bills are short-term securities with maturities of one year or less. Government securities, such as U.S. Treasury bills and bonds, offer a high degree of safety and are guaranteed as to the timely payment of principal and interest. Inflation is represented by the Consumer Price Index (CPI) and is a measure of change in consumer prices, as determined by the U.S. Bureau of Labor Statistics. Past performance cannot guarantee comparable future results.

WHAT DOES THIS DATA SUGGEST TO YOU?

Look at this Reward table and ask yourself: if you want to become a millionaire in 35 years, and you need to grow your money at 10% a year in order to do it, where do you need to invest your money?

Ownership investments such as stocks have historically done a much better job of growing your money compared to loanership investments such as bonds.

Historically, there has been no better investment for growing your money than investing in common stocks. Although past performance cannot guarantee future results, nothing has outperformed common stocks as an investment.

Ownership investments such as stocks have historically done a much better job of growing your money compared to loanership investments such as bonds.

Historically, there has been no better investment for growing your money than investing in common stocks. Although past performance cannot guarantee future results, nothing has outperformed common stocks as an investment.

THE PENALTY FOR "PLAYING IT SAFE"

Many people are reluctant to invest in ownership investments like stocks because they are fearful they will lose their money. They perceive them as "too risky". They remember the stock market crashes of 1929 and 1987, the protracted bear market declines like 1973-1974, and all the other negative-return years. They know that stock prices go up and down a lot, and they are uncomfortable experiencing this volatility when it comes to their own hard-earned capital.

So they put their money in Certificates of Deposit at the bank, or at best, in "risk-free" U.S. T-Bills, and they sleep much better at night knowing their money is "safe." And they wake up twenty years later and wonder why they can't afford to live on what they've worked so hard to save over all those years.

GOING BROKE SAFELY

You can call it "going broke safely." These people played it "safe" but it came back to haunt them because they didn't realize that Inflation the Money Monster was truly the beast that it is and inflicts the damage it does. By protecting themselves from principal risk in the *short*-term, they subject themselves to wealth risk in the *long*-run because over time the purchasing power of their principal erodes down to a fraction of what it once was. It's as if they received a steady series of pay cuts in their paychecks. One day they realize they can barely afford to live on what they are making, and sometimes it is too late to do anything about it. Can you see how "Playing It Safe" equates to "Going Broke Safely?"

The two tables which follow further illustrate this point. The first table shows the ending values you would achieve by investing $264 a month for 35 years in these investments at their historical average annual rates of return. The second table tells you how long it takes to become a millionaire investing $264 a month in each of the investments at their historical average annual rates of return.

Can you see how the penalty for playing it "safe" by investing in U.S. T-Bills is a huge price to pay compared to the "risky" investment in common stocks? The longer the time horizon, the bigger the penalty.

The rates of return are presented *before* accounting for inflation. When you subtract the historical average annual inflation rate of 3.1% from each of the investment rates of return, you get "real" rates of return of 0.7% for T-Bills, 2.2% for Government Bonds, and 7.9% for Stocks. These "real" rates of return give you your inflation-adjusted returns - how much you can expect your money to grow in terms of the purchasing power it will provide (or fail to provide) in the future.

Inflation adjustments aside, do you see how long it will take to become a millionaire investing entirely in U.S. T-Bills, investing $264 a month and growing your money an average 3.8% a year?

It will take 68 years. Add 68 to your present age and see how old you will be then. Are you willing to wait that long to become a millionaire? How important is "playing it safe" when it comes to the achievement of your long-term financial goals? Is "going broke safely" the path you want to take?

Again, there has been no better investment for growing your money than investing in common stocks. Historically, nothing has outperformed common stocks as an investment.

Risk, Reward, and The Penalty for Playing It "Safe"

This table shows you the difference over time of investing $264 a month for 35 years in various types of investments assuming their historical (1926 - 1997) average annual rates of return.

(Note: see page 90, **What You Need to Know About This Data**, in the *Reward* chapter, for important disclosures relative to this data).

	Rates of Return	Ending Values after 35 years
Smaller Company Stocks	12.7%	$2,051,290
Larger Company Stocks	11.0%	$1,301,070
Long-Term Government Bonds	5.3%	$320,724
U.S. Treasury Bills	3.8%	$231,189

How Long It Takes

This table shows you how long it takes to grow a million dollars investing $264 a month for 35 years in various types of investments assuming their historical (1926 - 1997) average annual rates of return.

(Note: see page 90, **What You Need to Know About This Data**, in the *Reward* chapter, for important disclosures relative to this data).

	Rates of Return	How Many Years it takes to grow into a Million Dollars
Smaller Company Stocks	12.7%	29
Larger Company Stocks	11.0%	33
Long-Term Government Bonds	5.3%	54
U.S. Treasury Bills	3.8%	68

Many people are reluctant to invest in common stocks because of the inherent price volatility. So they put their money in Certificates of Deposit at the bank, or at best, in "risk-free" U.S. T-Bills, and they sleep much better at night knowing their money is "safe." And they wake up twenty years later and wonder why they can't afford to live on what they've worked so hard to save over all those years.

By protecting themselves from principal risk in the *short*-term, they subject themselves to wealth risk in the *long*-run because over time the purchasing power of their principal erodes down to a fraction of what it once was.

Inflation the Money Monster will see to it that "Playing It Safe" equates to "Going Broke Safely".

Investing $264 a month entirely in U.S. T-Bills, "safely" growing your money an average 3.8% a year, it will take 68 years to become a millionaire.

AVERAGE ANNUAL RETURNS AND PAST PERFORMANCE

In virtually every discussion about investment returns you will find mandatory disclaimers about Average Annual Returns and Past Performance. Be sure you understand these two important concepts completely. They apply to every mention of investment returns in this book.

AVERAGE ANNUAL RETURNS

"Average Annual Returns" are just that: returns which are measured on an annual basis, averaged out over the period of time for which they are reported. An 11% average annual return for common stocks does NOT mean an investor earned 11% each and every year, year in and year out.

Indeed, over the course of the last 72 years there have been a number of years when the ending value of an investment in common stocks was *lower* than it was at the start of that year. These are *negative* return years: instead of growing the investment value at 11%, the investment actually declined in value!

In other years, that same investment increased in value substantially more than 11%.

When the declines and the increases are averaged over the period of time being measured, you get the Average Annual Return that is reported as such. There have been more positive return years than negative return years, but remember that these average annual returns are only *your* returns if you are invested from start to finish during the period being measured!

PAST PERFORMANCE: THE PAST IS NOT THE FUTURE

Past Performance in investment returns is never a guarantee of future performance in investment returns. No one can predict the future of investment returns in general or your investment returns in particular.

Past Performance is measurable but this does not automatically translate into Future Performance. The past may or may not be a good indicator of the future. Anything can happen in the future, and "anything" can change everything!

With nothing better to go on, we do turn to the measurable past to help us formulate our expectations for the future. The longer the history of the past performance being measured, the more comfortable we feel going forward that our future expectations may be met. No matter how comfortable you feel, however, always keep in mind that your own actual results may vary from past results.

Past Performance never guarantees Future Performance.

"Average Annual Returns" are merely averages of past annual returns.

Past Performance is never a guarantee of Future Performance.

THE PERFECT INVESTMENT

The Perfect Investment would have the following characteristics:

You can get in and out of the investment quickly and easily, and you will always get out of it at least as much as you put it into it. Your principal would be stable and *never* decline in value.

Your principal would earn regular interest at an interest rate which is higher than the rate of inflation. Your interest rate never fluctuates, and your interest income is guaranteed. The interest rate would be the absolute best you could find anywhere.

Your principal also grows at a consistent rate, which is also higher than inflation. The rate of growth does not fluctuate and is itself guaranteed. The rate of growth would also be the absolute best you could find anywhere. No other investment would outperform yours: it would be the best investment available anywhere in the world.

In summary, The Perfect Investment would be completely liquid and completely free of risk, and it would protect and preserve your principal, generate income for you, and grow in value each and every year you owned it.

By now you hopefully realize that although there may be a Santa Claus, there is no such thing as The Perfect Investment.

There is no such thing as The Perfect Investment.

IS THERE A RISK-FREE INVESTMENT?

Even though there is no such thing as the perfect investment, wouldn't it be wonderful to at least be able to find an investment that is free of risk?

Forget it. **There is no such thing as a risk-free investment.** There's no such thing as a risk-free life either. Every day you get up and go out into the world you face all kinds of risks. Does this prevent you from making a go of your life? If you built a cocoon around yourself and stayed inside it you would reduce a lot of risk but you'd also be missing out on all the opportunities for love, beauty, and happiness that a rich fulfilling life has to offer. There is no reward without some risk attached to it, in life and in investing.

Every investment in the universe carries with it some inherent risk.

Millions of people all over the world invest in securities issued by the United States Government. The short-term U.S. Treasury Bills (often called T-Bills) are perceived to be a risk-free investment. After all, they are issued by the United States Treasury and are backed by the full faith and credit of the United States Government. The day our government defaults on its debt obligations is likened to the day the world ends.

Indeed, T-Bills are free from nearly all of the risks described in the *Risk* chapter, most notably business risk and default risk. People feel secure investing in the debt obligations of our own federal government, the largest and "safest" debtor in the world. The fact that T-Bills mature in either three months, six months, or one year provides added comfort because you are constantly getting your money back.

But this same feature also highlights the first important risk you assume with this investment: Reinvestment risk. When interest rates decline, they decline for all loanership investments, including T-Bills. If interest rates are declining, you are forced into constantly rolling over your principal into investments that pay less and less in income to you.

The second and far more important risk you assume by investing in T-Bills is the greatest risk of all: Wealth risk. The very reason people invest in T-Bills - safety and security and freedom from most investment risk - is the very reason they are assuming the greatest risk of all.

So as great as the T-Bill is for a short-term loanership investment, it is not a risk-free investment! The returns you receive from investing primarily in T-Bills will do serious damage to your long-term wealth-building strategy and financial independence goal. You might still become a millionaire investing exclusively in T-Bills, but it will take a long, long, time.

Safety, security and freedom from risk simply does not pay very well (as you have learned in the *Reward* and *The Penalty for Playing it "Safe"* chapters).

There is no such thing as a Risk-Free Investment.

WHAT IS COMMON STOCK?

Common stock represents an ownership interest in a publicly-held company.

If you started your own business from scratch you would have a 100% ownership interest in your business, which is privately-held. You may build it up to the point where you bring in key people to help you manage the business, and maybe you give them or sell them some ownership interest in your business.

Although you may have retained a majority interest in your business, you no longer have a 100% ownership interest. The business is still privately-held, but now there are other owners with a vested interest in seeing that business prosper.

THE INITIAL PUBLIC OFFERING OF A COMPANY'S COMMON STOCK

As the business prospers the owners see a great deal more potential, but they decide they want to raise more money to invest in the continued growth of the company. One way to raise money is to divide the company into smaller ownership interests and sell these interests to the public. The original owners are giving up some of their ownership interest in the business in exchange for cash. They hire professionals (called investment bankers and underwriters) to advise them throughout the process, and to help them sell the new ownership interests to the public for the first time, which is called an Initial Public Offering (IPO). Once ownership is offered and sold to the public at large, it becomes a publicly-held company.

The ownership interests are represented by pieces of paper called stock certificates, or shares of stock. The company actually issues individual stock certificates which are numbered and used to keep track of all the registered owners of the company. Common stock is one of several different classes of stock the company could have issued, each class having its own rights and privileges. Common stockholders do not participate in the day-today management of the company, but management is accountable to them as owners of the company.

Common stockholders do have a voice in how the company is run in that they elect a Board of Directors to represent them in establishing corporate objectives and policies, and in choosing and advising the officers and managers of the company. Each stock certificate is equal to one vote. The more shares of stock one owns, the larger the ownership interest in the company one has.

THE SECONDARY MARKET, ALSO KNOWN AS THE STOCK MARKET

Beyond the Initial Public Offering, when the initial ownership interests were sold in exchange for the raising of the cash which the owners will now invest into further building the company, some people will want to sell their ownership interest and other people will want to buy an ownership interest. They do this in the stock market, which is considered the secondary market as opposed to the Initial Public Offering. The stock will be listed as officially trading on one of the major stock exchanges: the New York Stock Exchange, the American Stock Exchange, and the "over-the-counter" (OTC) Market, or NASDAQ, and this where you go, through a broker-dealer, to transact your business. Specialists at the Exchanges are assigned to ensure the stock will have a place in the market where buyers and sellers can be matched up.

There is a buyer and seller for every stock transaction (and it may be a dealer who "makes a market" in the security by buying and selling out of its own inventory). The company whose stock is being transacted is responsible for keeping track of its owners, and every time a stock certificate trades hands the new owner's name is recorded as the registered owner of that certificate.

HOW A STOCK'S TRADING PRICE IS DETERMINED

The price people pay or receive when they buy or sell their shares of stock is determined entirely by the free market forces which exist in any marketplace and is not set by the company or by anyone else. The price people paid at the Initial Public Offering has absolutely nothing to do with the price going forward. The company received cash in exchange for those initial shares, and that's all the cash they will receive. The only cash that changes hands now is entirely between the people buying and selling the shares in the secondary market.

The value of a share of stock in the marketplace is not the accounting value. The accounting value in the company is calculated by adding up all of the assets of the company and subtracting all of the liabilities to get a value called stockholders' equity, which is then divided by all of the outstanding shares of stock to get the "book value" or accounting value per share.

The market value of a share of stock is determined by what a willing buyer is willing to pay and what a willing seller is willing to sell for, which is obviously a matter of opinion. The opinion of market value is based upon what people think about the past performance, and the present and future prospects of the company. How well has the company's officers and managers grown its sales and earnings in the past, how is it doing currently, and more importantly, how well will it do going forward?

If the economy (or stock market) as a whole looks like it might be headed for trouble, this too will influence people's opinions about a company's prospects in the near future. In contrast, when the economy (or stock market) has been experiencing rough times but the future begins looking rosy again, people regain their lost confidence. For better or for worse, stock prices will reflect these opinions.

The bottom line is that the objective of any company's officers and managers is to create, maintain, and increase shareholder value. This value is measured by the stock price. The whole idea behind owning stock in a company is that your ownership interest will presumably grow in value over time, and your stock will be worth more than you paid for it.

AN EXAMPLE

If, when the company sold its first shares of stock for ten dollars a share it was generating one dollar a share in earnings, then people were willing to pay ten dollars for one dollar of earnings per share. As time went on and the company increased its sales of its products and services, and the company did it profitably so that its earnings also increased to, say, two dollars a share, the owners of those original shares have prospered. Their company is delivering twice the results it once did. This would attract the attention of other people who might also be interested in becoming a part owner of such a prosperous, productive company.

If people were willing to pay the equivalent of what you paid - ten dollars per dollar of earnings - they would pay twenty dollars per share for the current two dollars in earnings. Your original share, for which you paid ten dollars, could be sold on the open market for twenty dollars, or twice what you paid. This is a simplistic but representative example of how ownership interests in companies grow in value. As a company prospers and increases its sales and earnings over time, the company does become more valuable and consequently so does your ownership interest in it.

STOCK SPLITS

Often a company's stock grows so high in value the company may feel the price too prohibitive to attract prospective new investors. For example, if a stock has grown in value and a single share is currently priced at $100 a share, management may decide to "split the stock." It may decide to take each share of outstanding stock at $100 and split it into two shares, each now worth $50 a share. Every shareholder must trade in the old share certificate for two brand new certificates worth half as much. The value of your holdings remain exactly the same as they did before the split - $100 - but now you have two certificates instead of one. If the company was paying dividends on the shares, these will also be split so the total value of the dividends you receive from the new shares remains the same as before.

Stock splits are primarily a psychological maneuver. People seem to prefer using $100 to buy five shares of $20 stock to two shares at $50 to one share at $100. Truthfully, it's not the price per share that matters, it's what the company itself has done and is expected to continue doing that really matters. A part ownership in a mediocre company selling for $12 a share is a poor investment compared to a part ownership in an outstanding company selling for $75 a share.

Interestingly, the outstanding company is more likely to have been selling at $20 a share, grown it to $80, split it to make it more psychologically affordable, and then continue growing and splitting and growing and splitting. A long-time owner could end up with multiple quantities of shares compared to when she started, all of which have grown substantially in value and all of which generate increasing dividends as well.

Whether your own particular ownership interests increase or decrease in value, and how long it takes to do so, depends upon how well you choose the companies in which to invest, and how well those companies actually perform over time.

Whether your own particular ownership interests increase or decrease in value, and how long it takes to do so, depends upon how well you choose the companies in which to invest, and how well those companies actually perform over time.

WHAT IS A "BLUE CHIP" STOCK?

A "blue chip" stock is an ownership interest in a company which has a long and well-established track record of consistently growing its sales and earnings over time. How long is long? It's a matter of opinion but a fair time frame is twenty-five years or more.

Blue chip companies are considered to be the largest and best-managed companies in the country. It is not enough simply to be among the largest - it must also be considered to be among the best-managed.

You can find blue chip stocks in virtually every industry (providing the industry itself is at least twenty-five years old), and every industry may have more than just one blue chip company in it.

The blue chip companies are usually the ones with the largest market shares in their industry, meaning they are the industry leaders. The officers and managers have proven their commitment to increasing shareholder value as evidenced by the company's long-term track record of increasing sales and earnings.

HOW COMPANIES BECOME BLUE CHIPS

No company starts out being a blue chip company. They frequently start out as very small companies but they grow because they offer products and services that people want, and they offer them the way people want them. As more and more people want the company's products and services, the company's sales and earnings increase and the company grows in value and so does its stock price.

No one can accurately consistently predict which of today's small companies will grow into tomorrow's blue chip companies. Steadily increasing sales and market share is sometimes a good indicator, but only if earnings are following suit. Earnings do not always increase just because sales do. If management does a poor job of managing the money generated by sales, it's always possible the company can lose money even as its sales are growing. Blue chip companies do occasionally stumble and fall, and consequently so does its stock price, but these periods are usually infrequent and the companies usually regain their footing and get back on track.

Blue chip companies are considered to be mature companies, due to their long track records of proven performance. Past performance is never a guarantee of future performance, but a proven track record is often a fairly good measure of what could be expected in the future.

Blue chip companies have demonstrated their commitment to increasing shareholder value for many years, as evidenced by the company's stock price which has also risen consistently for many years. Remember, as a company grows more valuable over time so do the owners' interest in the company, and a share of stock in that company is worth more today than in the past.

One way management adds value to its stock price is by regularly sharing a part of the company's earnings directly with the owners. When a company is small it plows back all of its earnings right back into the company to keep it going and growing. It needs the earnings it generates to reinvest in itself with the hope that it will increase its market share in its industry and eventually emerge as one of the biggest and best-run companies in its industry. This takes time, and it takes a lot of increasing sales, and it takes good management to ensure consistent and increasing earnings are generated from those sales.

PAYING DIVIDENDS

As the company matures with proven success, management may feel confident that it can continue growing without having to plow back *all* of the company's earnings back into the company. Management decides it will begin to share a portion of the company's earnings directly with its owners, and it declares a dividend of some specific amount per share which the company actually pays out to its shareholders by writing a check for the amount of the dividend and sending it to each owner. This usually occurs on a quarterly basis.

For example, if the company generates a dollar a share in earnings and management declares a dividend of twenty-five cents a share, the company will retain seventy-five cents a share of those earnings to reinvest back into the company and it will pay out twenty-five cents a share for every share outstanding. As an owner of the company you will receive twenty-five cents for each and every share of stock you own.

As you might imagine, these dividends are well-regarded by many people. The dividends represent an immediate return on the owners' investment in the company. Even more importantly, as the company consistently grows its earnings, it continues to share a part of these earnings with the owners and these dividends also grow in time. The dividends become a steady source of income for people, and receiving the dividend may be the very reason they buy the stock.

Over time the blue chip companies not only demonstrate a long-term track record of consistently growing sales and earnings, they also build a long-term record of steadily increasing the dividends it pays out to shareholders. The stock price rises because of management's demonstrated ability to increase the value of the company. The owners benefit from a consistently rising stock price, and they benefit by regularly sharing in the earnings of their company by the dividends they receive, which should also increase over time.

Occasionally, when a blue chip company does stumble and fall by suffering a drop in either sales or earnings or both, management may decide it needs to cut or eliminate the dividend it has been paying (because it needs the money to try and recover) until such time as the future looks more secure. This is not well-regarded by anyone, and the stock price suffers. These events are an exception to the long-term proven track records (which makes it all the worse when it happens), but it does happen and it happens to some of the biggest and best-managed companies in the country. When it does happen, buy the stock! We'll learn more about this in the chapter entitled *When the Stock Market Has a Sale.*

By and large, blue chip companies and their stocks are highly desirable investments by those who invest in common stocks. Maturity and experience and consistent results are highly-valued in comparison to the inexperienced and untried and unproved.

The common stock of blue chip companies belongs in every "Millionaire in the Making"'s investment portfolio.

The common stock of blue chip companies belongs in every "Millionaire in the Making"'s investment portfolio.

WHAT IS THE STOCK MARKET AND WHERE IS WALL STREET?

When people talk about the stock market they're talking about the market for stocks in general, just as they talk about the real estate market, or automobile market, or job market. The stock market is measured chiefly by the performance of certain indexes that are widely accepted to be representative of the market for stocks as a whole.

In 1896 a man by the name of Charles Dow began tracking the stock prices of twelve of the largest companies in America at that time, including Distilling & Cattle Feeding, Tennessee Coal & Iron, and U.S. Rubber. He averaged the stock prices of all twelve companies, called it The Dow Jones Industrial Average, and published it for subscribers in what he called the *Customer's Afternoon Letter,* the forerunner of the *Wall Street Journal.*

The Dow Jones Industrial Average continues to be published today, and it is the most widely-followed index in the world. At its debut the initial value of the Dow Jones Industrial Average was $40.94. Measured today in "points" rather than dollars, and more than the simple average it once was, the index reached an all-time high (as of this writing) of 8,900 in March 1998.

The Dow Jones Industrial Average still only consists of thirty companies, which makes people wonder just how representative of the entire market it can truly be. Over the years the particular companies which comprise the index have been changed, at the sole discretion of the publishers of the index. You'll find the current list at the end of the chapter (it reflects the changes made in 1997). The only remaining company from the original list is General Electric.

There are thousands of publicly-held and publicly-traded companies in America today. A better representation of the stock market as a whole might be an index consisting of more than just thirty stocks. That's what the folks at Standard & Poors Corporation thought when they created the S&P 500. This broader index consists of 500 different companies instead of the Dow's 30. The S&P 500 contains many, many blue chip companies across a wide array of industries representing virtually every industry in the American economy. It too is a widely-followed and reported index. Interestingly and remarkably, the two indexes have tended to mirror each other over time.

Other indexes have been created throughout the years, and there are now dozens of them. The Russell 2000, for example, consists of 2000 stocks of smaller companies, and the Wilshire 5000 has 5000 companies of every size in it. There are bond indexes too, and there are indexes measuring stock markets all over the world.

A WALK DOWN WALL STREET

The famous Wall Street in New York City allegedly got its name from a wall that was originally built around it to ensure business could be conducted without outside interference.

The merchants and brokers of the day agreed they needed a central location for buying and selling securities, and they formalized their agreement in a document they called the "Buttonwood Agreement," so named because they formed it under a buttonwood tree. Out of this agreement emerged the New York Stock Exchange which officially began operations in 1792. From the Buttonwood Agreement to this very day, only members can trade there. Anyone wishing to buy or sell securities must go through a member of the New York Stock Exchange, located at 68 Wall Street. There is a fixed number (1,366) of memberships, called seats, on the Exchange. A seat on the Exchange cost $4,000 in 1876, $625,000 before the crash of 1929, $25,000 in the 1940's,

$665,000 in the roaring bull market of the late 1980's, and reached an all-time high of $2,000,000 on March 9, 1998.

Today there are more than 3,000 stocks which trade on the New York Stock Exchange, and each company must meet certain Exchange requirements in order to have their stock listed and traded there. The majority of blue chip companies' stocks trade on the New York Stock Exchange. Companies who do not meet the requirements (or choose not to be listed there) will have their stock trade on either the American Stock Exchange, or the "over-the-counter" (OTC) market, also known as NASDAQ. NASDAQ is not an exchange with a precise physical location but rather a network of broker-dealers all connected to each other by a sophisticated computer network, with trading rights and privileges assigned accordingly. There are also a number of regional stock exchanges located throughout the country.

When you place your order to buy or sell a stock, you always go through a broker-dealer through whom you've established an account. You may not even know where the stock is listed or where it trades, and if it does trade on the New York Stock Exchange, your broker-dealer may or may not have its own seat on the Exchange. If it does not, the broker-dealer will have an arrangement with one or more members through which it will transact trades. All you may ever know is the name of the company whose stock you want to buy or sell, and the total amount of the transaction.

You will pay a commission to the broker-dealer for every purchase and every sale, and these commissions vary substantially from one broker-dealer to the next (and they often vary depending upon the size of the transaction). The transaction itself, if placed as a "market order" which means whatever the current market price is at the moment, only takes seconds to execute regardless of how and where the trade is placed. The entire securities industry continues to make a concerted effort to ensure the individual investor is accorded the same (or better) treatment as the institutional investor.

Now that you know a little more about the stock market and Wall Street we can continue our discussion about investing in common stocks.

You can become a Millionaire without ever walking down Wall Street.

The Dow Jones Industrial Average

This is a current listing of the 30 companies whose stock prices comprise the Dow Jones Industrial Average.
How many of these names do you recognize?

Alcoa	International Business Machines (IBM)
AlliedSignal	International Paper
American Express	J.P. Morgan
AT&T	Johnson & Johnson
Boeing	McDonald's
Caterpillar	Merck
Chevron	Minnesota Mining & Manufacturing (3M)
Coca-Cola	Philip Morris
Dupont	Proctor & Gamble
Eastman Kodak	Sears
Exxon	Travelers
General Electric	Union Carbide
General Motors	United Technologies
Goodyear	Wal-Mart
Hewlett-Packard	Walt Disney

HOW RISKY ARE COMMON STOCKS?

We've discussed the fact that there is no such thing as a risk-free investment, we've demonstrated the penalty for playing it safe, and we've presented common stocks as an alternative which offers great long-term rewards in exchange for the necessary assumption of corresponding risk. The proper question to ask now is: How risky are common stocks?

In 1973 the stock market declined by 15%. For every $1,000 you started with, you closed the year with only $850. In 1974 the stock market declined another 27%. Your $850 was only worth $621 at the end of the second year. In 1975 the market rebounded and returned 37%, and your $621 went back up to $850. Even so, over the course of three entire years your stock portfolio ended lower than when you started!

Who in their right mind would make this kind of investment? Who in their right mind would sit tight through an entire year in which the value of their investment holdings declines, month after month, before their very eyes? And if they did sit tight that first year, who in their right mind would sit tight through an entire second year of continuing declines in their investment holdings?

Month after month of continuing market declines the "gloom and doomsters" have been blaring their trumpets with screaming headlines about the end of the investment world as we know it. Indeed, looking at 1973 through 1976, it would take four years to barely break even on your investments. Who in their right mind would remain invested throughout the entire four years, and who in their right mind would ever invest in common stocks again?

Intelligent long-term investors, that's who! Millionaires in the Making, every one of them. Why?

There has been no better investment for growing your money than investing in common stock. Historically nothing has outperformed common stocks as an investment.

These things happen. We *expect* them to happen! There are going to be bumps in the road, but knowing you're going to hit them shouldn't keep you from driving. Stock market declines come with the territory and there is no escaping them, unless you want to play it "safe" and avoid the territory altogether. We've seen *that* alternative and we know it's not much of an alternative.

A LOOK BACK IN TIME

Look at the chart of Annual Returns for the Stock Market for the past 72 years, as measured by the annual returns of the S&P 500 (found at the end of this chapter). If you count up the number of negative-return years you'll discover 20 of them. If you count up the number of positive-return years you'll find there were 52. This implies that in any given year you would have had a 72% chance of making money in the stock market, and a 28% chance of losing money.

Although the number of positive-return years far exceeds the number of negative-return years, no one knows in advance when the negative-return years are going to show up. Also, the returns are never exactly the same from one year to the next, and no one knows in advance to what degree the return will be positive or negative. Of the total 72 years, 30 of the years had returns that were less than 10%, (including the negative returns), and 42 of the years had returns exceeding 10% (in 29 of them, the returns exceeded 20%).

So although there is a lot of uncertainty, (which, as you recall, is another word for risk), about investing in common stocks, because no one knows in advance what specific return we will experience in any given year, we do know that: 1) For more than seventy years, the average annual return for common stocks is more than 10% a year, and 2) Historically nothing has outperformed common stocks as an investment.

If you analyze the historical annual returns of the S&P 500 a little further, you would discover that if you took any rolling five-year period of time and averaged the returns, you would have had a 90% chance of making money and a 10% chance of losing money. Over any rolling ten-year period, your odds of a positive-return year were 93% versus 7% for a negative return. If you owned stocks in any of the rolling fifteen-year periods of the 72-year history, you would have had a 100% chance of making money in the stock market. Of course the past is no guarantee for the future, and furthermore it is not possible to actually invest in the S&P 500 index, so people's actual experiences will vary, but as the S&P 500 serves as a proxy for investing in stocks, the analysis is very enlightening.

HOW RISKY ARE COMMON STOCKS?

If you measure risk as the chance you might lose money, in the short run they are very risky. The longer you remain invested, the lower the risk and the greater the likelihood of positive results. In the short run the volatility *could* do some serious damage to your principal. In the long run, Inflation the Money Monster *will* do some serious damage to your principal. In the long run, historically, nothing has outperformed common stocks as an investment.

If you choose to become a millionaire by growing your money an average of 10% a year, and you have at least ten years of growing money in front of you, then common stocks should be your primary investment vehicle. If you want the Reward you must accept the necessary Risk.

Stock ownership among the general public has doubled in the past 7 years, according to a survey commissioned by the National Association of Securities Dealers (the NASD). Forty-three percent of U.S. adults now own shares in public companies, compared to 21% in 1990 and 10% in 1965. (Source: *Deloitte & Touche Review*, March 17, 1997).

Of course the 1990s (to date) has been a particularly outstanding period of time to own stocks as we have not experienced a significant market setback since the great market meltdown of October 1987. What will these new investors do in the face of such adversity when it strikes again? Will they panic and jump off the ship, or will they remain calm and stay the course? It matters far less what "they" do. All that matters is what you do. As a long-term investor you can be sure you will have plenty of opportunity to experience market setbacks, so you may as well prepare yourself for them.

If you measure risk as the chance you might lose money, in the short run common stocks are very risky. In the long run, historically, nothing has outperformed common stocks as an investment.

If you choose to become a millionaire by growing your money an average of 10% a year, and you have at least ten years of growing money in front of you, then common stocks should be your primary investment vehicle.

As a long-term investor you can be sure you will have plenty of opportunity to experience market setbacks, so you may as well prepare yourself for them.

If you want the Reward you must accept the necessary Risk.

Annual Stock Market Returns

Here is a year by year listing of stock market returns as measured by the S&P 500, assuming reinvestment of dividends. Parentheses around numbers indicate negative-return years in which market values declined.

1926	11.60	1951	24.02	1976	23.61
1927	37.57	1952	18.35	1977	(7.40)
1928	43.58	1953	(0.98)	1978	6.52
1929	(8.44)	1954	52.62	1979	18.48
1930	(24.89)	1955	31.57	1980	32.48
1931	(43.36)	1956	6.56	1981	(4.95)
1932	(8.09)	1957	(10.78)	1982	21.55
1933	53.81	1958	43.36	1983	22.56
1934	(1.36)	1959	11.96	1984	6.27
1935	47.61	1960	0.47	1985	31.73
1936	33.96	1961	26.82	1986	18.67
1937	(35.02)	1962	(8.75)	1987	5.25
1938	31.09	1963	22.65	1988	16.61
1939	(0.41)	1964	16.39	1989	31.69
1940	(9.77)	1965	12.35	1990	(3.11)
1941	(11.60)	1966	(10.06)	1991	30.47
1942	20.29	1967	23.95	1992	7.62
1943	25.98	1968	11.08	1993	10.08
1944	19.72	1969	(8.47)	1994	1.33
1945	36.45	1970	3.99	1995	37.58
1946	(8.08)	1971	14.32	1996	22.96
1947	5.72	1972	18.94	1997	33.36
1948	5.50	1973	(14.80)		
1949	18.79	1974	(26.49)		
1950	31.72	1975	37.27		

WHEN THE STOCK MARKET HAS A SALE

Although we know that no other investment category has outperformed common stocks for the last seventy-plus years, we also know that the stock market never goes straight up. The 11% average annual return is an average of ALL of the ups and downs over all of the years.

There are peaks and valleys and you can count on them just as you can count on the expansions and recessions of the business cycles within our economy. There are, as we have seen, negative-return years in which the value of your investments declines. Sometimes when it's bad, it's really bad, and the media won't hesitate to tell everybody how bad it really is. This instills fear in people. Fear sells newspapers and magazines and television broadcasts. Fear feeds on itself and spreads like wildfire. Fear is a very powerful emotion and it frequently causes people to act irrationally.

YOU HAVEN'T LIVED UNTIL YOU'VE EXPERIENCED A BEAR MARKET

If you define a bear market as one in which the stock market (as measured by the S&P 500) declines in value by 15% or more, in the past 45 years we have had 14 such bear markets. The average length of time the market declined in these bear markets was 8 months. The average loss of market value in these bear markets was 24%. The average length of time it took to recover from these bear markets was 13 months. (Source: Van Kampen

American Capital, 1997, *Bulls? Bears? How Much Do You Really Have To Care?*). "Average" means there were bear markets which never quite reached all of these numbers, and there were bear markets which exceeded all of these numbers.

The way to overcome fear about market declines is to think of them as the opportunities of a lifetime.

Ignore the media. When they tell you it's bad, tell yourself it's really good! Think of market declines as the stock market offering a sale on some of the best merchandise in the store! The stock market is the only place I know that when they have a sale everybody runs out of the store.

Do you run out of a store when there's a sale on your favorite merchandise? Why should the stock market be any different?

BE BRAVE, BE PATIENT

When stock prices fall, think of it as a buying opportunity! Whatever the reason that caused the big sell-off of stocks and prices to fall, it's almost always a short-term aberration - a temporary deviation from the normal and usual course. "Short-term" can be anywhere from nine months to eighteen months to, as in the case of the severe 1973-1974 bear market, three years. (It took the third year - 1975 - to restore prices to their original levels).

Granted, it takes lots of courage to buy when everybody else seems to be selling. Especially when you are in the midst of a big decline in value, which is typically caused by a crisis of some sort or another. In 1973 it was the Oil Embargo and fear of inflation spiraling out of control. In 1987 it was a major market meltdown - Black Monday, with one of the largest single-day market declines in history. In 1990 it was the Gulf War and the start of an economic recession, and in 1994 it was interest rates increasing seven times in a single year. Whatever the reason, crisis is at hand, the fear-mongering media is predicting, in essence, the end of the world, and everybody flees from the stock market (and all of its inherent "risk") like there's no tomorrow, taking their money with them.

So yes, it takes a great deal of courage to block out the blaring trumpets of the "gloom-and-doomster" crowd, to look past the crisis of the day, to fight your way into the store when everybody's pushing, kicking and screaming to get out, and to part with your hard-earned capital to buy the stock that everybody else at the time believes is virtually worthless.

Whether it's trumpeted by the alleged market pundits as a normal "correction," a "crash," a "meltdown," or the "biggest single-day drop in prices in stock market history," you would do well to view the raging headlines as advertisements for a grand sale. It may be a "10%-off" sale, a "25%-off sale," or "the biggest sale in stock market history." You get to buy your favorite merchandise at a discount. Stock up!

THE REWARD FOR COURAGE AND PATIENCE

It takes courage, but eventually you will be rewarded. When the sale is over everybody returns to the best store in town and continues paying full price for the same top-quality merchandise you've been buying on sale all this time. Occasionally the pendulum swings the other way. People want to own stocks so badly they'll pay ridiculous prices to do so, and the market becomes over-valued. Now they're all fighting each other to get *in* to the store! Soon reality sets in, or another crisis will hit, and the crowd comes to its senses, but the pendulum never tops right in the middle. It swings the other way, to the other extreme as the market crashes once again. And there you are once again in the midst of a rare sale and extraordinary buying opportunity!

Fear and Greed drive the stock market and stock prices in the short term. The herd mentality feeds on the frenzy and runs over the edge and falls off the cliff together as a herd. Fundamental

Value drives the stock market and stock prices in the long-term. Fundamental Value is the ability to generate and increase sales and profits consistently over time. Don't be a part of the herd. If you believe in the companies in which you are a part-owner to continue to sell their existing products and create new ones to sell, all over the world, as they've been doing consistently for decade after decade, you have nothing to be afraid of.

PUT IT IN PERSPECTIVE

Do you think people will ever stop buying cereal, soap, toilet paper, newspapers, razors, shoes, drugs, gasoline, refrigerators, computers, cars, etc.? They might hold back temporarily on some of the discretionary items until the crisis of the day blows over, but they'll continue buying the staples. Crisis or not, they'll keep paying their gas, electric, and phone bills month after month, won't they?

And speaking of bills, are your bills lower today than they were ten or twenty years ago? How much more are you paying for the same items today compared to ten and twenty years ago? Wouldn't you like these people to be paying you, as part-owner of the companies raising the prices, more and more money over time? Wouldn't you like to be a part-owner of the companies from whom people all over the world are buying their goods and services?

Visualize a child rolling a yo-yo up and down its string and walking up a flight of stairs. The yo-yo goes up and it goes down, stair by stair. As the child climbs each stair, the yo-yo goes higher than it did on the previous stair, and when it rolls down it doesn't roll as low as it did on the previous stair. All the way up the stairs, you will notice that the highs are higher than they were before, and even the lows are higher than they were.

So it is with the stock market. People spend too much watching the yo-yo roll down on a single stair, as they spend too much time watching stock prices in a single year. If you are a long-term investor you must spend your time evaluating the whole staircase and appreciating the big picture.

If you look at a mountain chart depicting the stock market's historical returns side by side year after year, you'll see how the peaks of the mountain get higher and higher from left to right - from earlier years to later years. You'll see the mountain with jigs and jags, with peaks and valleys. The stock market never goes straight up, smoothly, year after year. It does go down, like the yo-yo on a string. But if you put your left finger on one of the earlier mountain chart peaks and you put your right finger on another peak ten years later, you will most likely find that your right finger is higher up the mountain than your left finger. Do the same with the valleys in-between the peaks. Over time, the highs go higher, and even the lows go higher.

So there are always stock market declines, and some of them are severe, but they never last as long as the long, steady upward climb the market has delivered for the last seventy-plus years. When the market has a sale, do not run out of the store with the rest of the herd. Be intelligent, be courageous, be a buyer at the sale. Especially when it's the best merchandise in the world - ownership in a blue chip company.

Remember, blue chip companies are among the largest and best-run companies in the country. They are the giants and market leaders in their industries. They are not about to disappear like a fly-by-night shoestring operation. They do occasionally make mistakes, fall short of their objectives, and fail to live up to Wall Street's expectations, and the stock prices suffers accordingly.

Sometimes it takes several years for a company to recover and for the stock price to rebound, so in addition to courage it takes time and patience on your part as you wait out the recovery. As a "Millionaire in the Making" you already have courage, time and patience. Take advantage of opportunity when it knocks on your door.

The stock market never goes straight up. The 10% average annual return is an average of ALL of the ups and downs over all of the years. There are stock market declines, and some of them are severe.

Think of market declines as the stock market offering a sale on some of the best merchandise in the store - ownership in blue chip companies, the largest and best-run companies in the country.

When the stock market has a sale, do not run out of the store with the rest of the herd.

Fear and Greed drive the stock market and stock prices in the short term. Fundamental Value drives the stock market and stock prices in the long-term.

Courage and patience in the stock market can reap huge financial rewards. Take advantage of opportunity when it knocks on your door.

WHAT IS A MUTUAL FUND?

Up until now we have discussed how an aspiring millionaire investing in common stocks could have historically achieved the targeted average annual return of 10% or better. We are now going to expand this discussion to include mutual funds as a way to invest in common stocks. The next three chapters are all about mutual funds.

You learned in the Risk chapters that the best way to manage investment risk is to spread out your exposure to individual risks as much as possible in order to reduce your exposure to any single risk. This is called diversification.

When you buy common stock you can pick and choose the particular companies in which you'd like to become a part owner. You find a brokerage firm, open an account, deposit some cash, place your order, pay your commission, and it's official - you're now one of the owners of the companies of your choice.

As a beginning investor starting from scratch, you may only be able to afford to buy into one company at a time. If all you have are one or two stocks in your portfolio, you are putting your hard-earned capital at the risk that those one or two companies will continue to perform as expected. And they may well do so. But what happens if they do not? Remember, even the beloved blue chips occasionally stumble. What happens if one of your holdings stumbles? There goes 100% of your portfolio in the case of owning one stock, or 50% if you own two. (Yes, it's a buying opportunity, but you also want as much of your money growing as much as possible). It's like owning that window with a single pane of glass in it. If a ball comes crashing through your window unexpectedly, your entire window is destroyed.

DIVERSIFY!

But what if you and your friends decided to get together and pool your investment dollars together and buy stocks together? You can keep track of who puts how much money into the pool and what percentage of the total each one of you owns. The larger your pool of money, the greater the number of stocks you can buy. Now your window has many smaller panes of glass in it, each pane protected by its own frame. If a ball comes crashing through, it may only take out one or two of the panes, leaving the rest of your window intact.

A mutual fund, by law, cannot invest any more than 5% of the total pool in any single company, which means the pool must own at least 20 companies. It is rare to find a mutual fund with only 20 holdings in it. A typical mutual fund holds dozens of companies, often well over a hundred.

This is known as diversification. You are spreading out your exposure to risk by spreading out your investment dollars across a number of different companies, reducing your dependency on any single one of them. If the fund holds one hundred stocks and one or two of them stumble, the impact on the whole pool is not as significant as if you were holding only two stocks and one of them stumbled.

This is not to say that the value of the whole pool is always rising. Whatever affects the stock market as a whole will affect the different pools investing in the stock market.

HIRE PROFESSIONALS

A mutual fund is a professional company which invests pools of people's money. The fund keeps track of who puts in how much money and how much the whole pool is worth on any given day and how much each person's particular percentage of the whole pool is worth. The fund hires professionals to pick and choose which companies the fund will own. These professional money managers have the experience, expertise, technology, research staffs, and other resources available to them to assist them in their investment decisions. You would expect these professionals to do a better job than you could do on your own, and they usually do.

THE STRUCTURE OF A MUTUAL FUND

When you invest in a mutual fund, you receive shares in exchange for your investment dollars and you become part owner of that mutual fund. As the fund pools together your money and the money of all the other shareholders, it buys shares of stock of all the different companies it selects for its portfolio, and all of the owners of the mutual fund become part owners of all of the companies the fund owns. As an owner you share in the risk and reward, the gains and losses, of the underlying investments of the mutual fund.

If you were investing on your own, your investment dollars may have only afforded you part ownership (and 100% risk) in a single company's stock. Those same dollars invested in a mutual fund gets you part ownership in dozens and dozens of companies' stocks (and spreads out your risk accordingly).

The great majority of mutual funds operate as open-end mutual funds, meaning the total number of shares in the fund is open-ended. When you buy and sell mutual fund shares you do so directly with the mutual fund itself. When you want to buy shares in a mutual fund you contact the fund itself (or your financial advisor who contacts the fund on your behalf) and place your order. The fund will issue as many shares as your investment dollars can buy at the current price. When you sell, also known as "redeem," the mutual fund buys the shares back from you directly, at whatever the current price is at the time of redemption, which may be more or less than what you paid when you invested.

DIFFERENT FUNDS HAVE DIFFERENT INVESTMENT OBJECTIVES

The mutual fund hires professionals to explore all of the investment alternatives available and select the ones they feel would perform the best for the objective at hand. When a mutual fund is established it will declare what its investment objective is. Not all mutual funds invest exclusively in common stock. Some funds have as their objective **the generation of income**, so it will pool money and only buy bonds. Some may specialize in only buying government bonds, some only corporate bonds, some only foreign bonds, and some will buy whatever bonds it feels will do the job.

Some funds will have **the growth of capital** as its objective, and choose to invest in stocks, but this can be accomplished in a myriad of ways and the fund may specialize in any one or more of them. Some funds will only invest in smaller companies, some only in the larger blue chip companies. Some will invest only in a certain sector of the economy like technology, or a certain industry like utilities. Some funds choose to invest only in companies outside of the United States.

Some funds have as its objective **both growth and income**. They may invest in bonds for interest income, blue chip stocks for dividend income with growth as a secondary objective, and other stocks purely for the growth potential. They may invest all over the world to try to accomplish its objective.

THE LEGAL REQUIREMENTS OF MUTUAL FUNDS

The mutual fund is an industry unto itself, and a huge industry at that. There are more than eight thousand mutual funds available.

There are more mutual funds than there are publicly-held company stocks available! Mutual funds are regulated by law just like other publicly-held companies. One of the legal requirements is that a mutual fund must publish a prospectus which details nearly everything there is to know about the fund, and every potential investor in the fund must receive a prospectus before becoming a shareholder.

The mutual fund is also required by law to send a semi-annual and an annual report to every owner of the fund. Every six months shareholders receive an accounting from the fund's managers which includes performance results, financial statements, and a discussion from management on their results and outlook. In addition, the report will provide a detailed listing of every holding in the portfolio, grouped by industry, so you can see exactly which companies the fund owns, how much of each company it owns, and what percentage of the total portfolio each holding represents.

If the fund owns it, you own it too! As a mutual fund shareholder, you become part-owner of dozens and dozens of companies in many different industries and sectors of the economy. If the professional managers are doing their jobs, you will own a piece of some the best companies in the country (and if the fund invests outside of the United States, you become part-owner of companies all over the world).

Upon your request every mutual fund company will be delighted to send you a copy of the prospectus, most recent semi-annual report, and general information on every fund of interest to you. They want you as a shareholder and they work very hard at earning and keeping your business. All the information is free of charge to you, so take advantage of it.

WHO INVESTS IN MUTUAL FUNDS?

Responding to the previously-referenced survey commissioned by the National Association of Securities Dealers (NASD), nearly half of the investors who said they own common stocks own them entirely through mutual funds. Investing in mutual funds has tripled over the last seven years, from 13% of U.S. adults in 1990 to 40% in 1997. (Source: *Deloitte & Touche Review*, March 17, 1997). The Investment Company Institute reported that the combined assets of the nation's mutual funds were $4.3 trillion in October 1997. Of this amount, $2.3 trillion was held by mutual funds invested in common stock.

Do you know how much 2.3 trillion dollars is? It's 2,300 billion dollars! This is an incredible amount of capital, yet every dollar of it is invested in common stock with the belief that it will grow and become more valuable in the future than it is today.

Owning a single company's stock is like owning a window with a single pane of glass in it. Owning a mutual fund is like owning a window with many panes of glass in it.

If your mutual fund owns it, you own it too! As a mutual fund shareholder, you become part-owner of dozens and dozens of companies in many different industries.

Professional money managers have the experience, expertise, technology, research staffs, and other resources available to them to assist them in their investment decisions. You would expect them to do a better job than you could do on your own.

WHY INVEST IN MUTUAL FUNDS?

You already know from the previous chapter two of the most important reasons for investing in mutual funds as a way to grow your money:

Diversification. You get instant diversification because the very nature and purpose of a mutual fund is to pool together the investment capital of large numbers of people and invest it in a large number of companies. It would take a great deal of your own money to put together the diverse portfolio that can be found in any mutual fund.

Again, no mutual fund is allowed to invest more than 5% of its total portfolio in any one investment, so at an absolute minimum every mutual fund will hold at least 20 different investments. If the fund limited its exposure to 2% in any given investment, it would have at least 50 different investments. The vast majority of mutual funds hold dozens and dozens of different investments, and many of these individual investments represent less than 1% of the fund's total portfolio.

Professional Management. Every mutual fund employs full-time professionals to assemble and manage the portfolio. These experienced well-paid professionals carefully research the companies in which they are considering investing, often meeting directly with the management of the companies to learn firsthand what management believes is in store for their respective company. The mutual fund managers make their buying (and selling) decisions based upon their careful research, analysis and experienced judgment. They carefully monitor and adjust the portfolio over time in response to changes at the individual companies in which they've invested (and the effect of the changes on the companies' stock prices), changes in market conditions, and changes in the economy as a whole.

Diversification and professional management are two major benefits of mutual funds. Other important benefits of investing in mutual funds are:

Small minimum purchases. Mutual fund investing is amazingly affordable. It takes very little money to assemble a diversified, professionally-managed portfolio of common stocks and/or bonds. The minimum amount a mutual fund will accept for an initial investment in the fund varies from fund to fund, but they range from as low as $250 or $500 to a typical minimum of $1,000. Additional investments must be made with minimums of $50 or $100, depending upon the fund.

BUILDING WEALTH WITH $50 A MONTH

Many funds will waive the initial minimum requirement altogether if you agree to make regular monthly investments by automatic bank draft from your checking or savings account! Depending upon the particular fund, the agreed-upon monthly investment can be as low as $50 a month, and some accept as little as $25 a month. Imagine becoming a part-owner of dozens and dozens of some of the biggest and best-run companies in the world with as little as $50 a month.

Automatic Reinvestment of Earnings. When a mutual fund owns stock in companies which pay dividends to its shareholders, the mutual fund is required by law to pass the dividends through to its own shareholders. The same holds true for all interest income it receives on the bonds its owns. At least once a quarter, the fund will add up all the dividend and interest it receives from all the companies it owns, and pay it out to the fund's shareholders. In addition, as the fund buys and sells investments throughout the year, it is required to add up all the profits and losses from its trades and pass along the net profit to its shareholders at least once a year. Many funds do this annually, typically in November or December, and it is called a capital gains distribution.

Instead of receiving your earnings in the form of a check, you can instruct the mutual fund to reinvest your dividends, interest, and capital gains back into the mutual fund and buy additional shares with the money you earned. These new shares will then be entitled to receive future earnings of their own, and you will be amazed at how quickly and beautifully your portfolio grows. It puts the Miracle of Compounding to work on your behalf, and over time the cumulative effect is substantial.

Shareholder Services. The mutual funds have large staffs of friendly professionals who are dedicated to the service and satisfaction of the fund's owner-shareholders (and prospective shareholders), and they are available via toll-free telephone numbers to respond immediately to inquiries and requests for service.

In addition to marketing brochures and the legal prospectuses, many mutual funds offer an assortment of free educational materials to help people understand basic investing concepts and the merits of investing through mutual funds. You are encouraged to take advantage of these resources.

Liquidity and Ease of Transacting Business. You can buy and sell shares of mutual funds on any given business day, and you can do it by mail or, once the account is established accordingly, by telephone.

Easy Access to Information. You can learn anything and everything there is to learn about any mutual fund in existence.

Because they are publicly-traded securities, mutual funds are regulated by law and must meet certain minimum standards regarding both the availability of timely information and the manner in which information is accurately reported to the public. So information is available directly from the mutual fund itself; simply call the toll-free number and request it.

You can also get your information from outside sources. Daily share prices and year-to-date returns, for example, are published daily in newspapers across the country. There are many other outside services (Morningstar, Lipper, CDA Wiesenberger, etc.) which track mutual fund performance, and although this information is offered by paid subscription, you can usually get it free of charge if you look for it. Our local library subscribes to Morningstar, for example, and you can search the Internet for the numerous web sites dedicated to mutual fund investing. Finally, every month dozens of magazines publish articles and performance records of mutual funds, and the major newspapers run more detailed listings after the close of each calendar quarter.

There is certainly no lack of information on mutual funds. If anything, there may be too much information, especially for the beginning investor. Let's explore the universe of mutual funds to get an overview of using mutual funds as your Millionaire investment vehicle.

The benefits of investing in mutual funds are:

Diversification	**Professional Management**
Affordable	**Systematic Investment**
Reinvestment of Earnings	**Liquid**
Shareholder Services	**Information Widely Available**

"WILL I LOSE ALL MY MONEY?"

This question occasionally arises from first-time mutual fund investors. If you have never invested in anything other than a Certificate of Deposit down at your local bank, something as "new" and "foreign" as investing in mutual funds always prompts a bit of fear and apprehension. You work hard for your money and you don't want to lose it.

To be sure, mutual funds are NOT deposits or any other obligations of any bank, nor of the government. Mutual funds are NOT insured by the FDIC or any other government agency. Mutual funds are NOT in any way guaranteed by any bank, or by the government. Mutual funds ARE subject to investment risks, including possible loss of the principal amount invested in them.

Is it possible to lose money investing in mutual funds? Yes, it is. Just as it is possible to lose money investing in common stocks. We have given a lot of attention to discussing Risk and Reward.

Is it possible to lose *all* of your money investing in mutual funds? The best way to answer the question is to take a look at the actual investments inside of a mutual fund portfolio. Every mutual fund is required by law to provide a detailed accounting of the fund, including all of its investments, to its shareholders and any interested member of the public. It does this in the form of the annual and semi-annual report it distributes. Once you become a shareholder in the fund you will receive these automatically. However anyone can call up any fund and request its latest report and the fund will gladly mail one to you.

Look at the Portfolio Listing which follows. It's a partial list of the actual investments held by a mutual fund which invests in blue chip companies. The investment objective of this fund is Growth and Income, so the fund invests in blue chips which it believes will continue growing, and the income comes from the dividends paid by these same blue chip companies.

Many people are amazed when they see how long these companies have been paying dividends. Depending upon your age, you can find companies which have been in business and paying out dividends to its shareholders long before you were born, long before your parents were born, before your grandparents were born, and even before your great-grandparents were born.

The only way you will lose *all* of your money investing in any mutual fund is for *all* of the individual investments held within the portfolio to lose *all* of their value. Virtually every mutual fund which has Growth and Income as its investment objective will contain Blue Chip companies like the ones listed here. These Blue Chip companies are among the biggest, longest-operating, best-managed, most valuable companies in America and in the world.

As a shareholder in the mutual fund you become part-owner of all of the companies in which your mutual fund invests. Your ownership interest grows more valuable as the companies themselves grow more valuable. As the companies pay out dividends each quarter, your mutual fund passes along your share of these dividends (although most people instruct their mutual funds to reinvest them back into the fund by buying more shares of the fund).

As part-owner of companies such as these, you prosper every time people turn on a light switch, make a phone call, fill up their gas tank, use a piece of tape, take a picture, make a photocopy, use a credit card, eat a bowl of cereal, fill a prescription, take an aspirin, put on a Band-Aid, reach for a tissue, shave, brush their teeth, wash their hands, hair, or dishes, etc., etc., etc. Millions and millions of people all over the world are using the products and services of "your" companies each and every day, and they use them day after day, week after week, month after month, year after year, and decade after decade.

When you add up all of the outstanding shares of stock in these companies and multiply them by the current price per share, you will learn that these companies are worth billions and billions of dollars. (This is their market value. See the "Market Value" column in the portfolio listing at the end of this chapter for examples of what some blue chip companies were worth in 1997).

The companies are worth so much because they generate billions and billions of dollars in sales and earnings, year after year after year. (The "Sales" column in the portfolio listing is an estimate of the billions of dollars of their goods and services these companies were expected to sell in 1997).

The day you will lose all of the money you have invested in companies like these is the day they all go out of business and become absolutely worthless.

As you look at the portfolio listing which follows, keep in mind that this list is simply a snapshot of the portfolio at a particular point in time. The actual portfolio will change as the portfolio managers decide to sell some of the investments and buy others. This list is only a partial list: the entire portfolio consists of many more holdings.

The dividend information is as of 1997. (*Source*: American Funds' Washington Mutual Investors Fund, July 31, 1997). Market values change daily, and sales estimates are just that: estimates. All dollars in the chart are rounded to the nearest billion. When reviewing the list, also remember that it is presented solely to illustrate a point, not to recommend specific investments.

As a shareholder in a mutual fund you become part-owner of all of the companies in which your mutual fund invests. Your ownership interest grows more valuable as the companies themselves grow more valuable.

Millions and millions of people all over the world are using the products and services of "your" companies each and every day, and they use them day after day, week after week, month after month, year after year, and decade after decade.

The day you will lose all of the money you have invested in them is the day they all go out of business and become absolutely worthless.

A Blue Chip Mutual Fund Portfolio

This is a partial listing of the actual investments held in the portfolio of a mutual fund which invests in Blue Chip companies, as of July 31, 1997.

	Dividends		1997 Estimates, in ***Billions*** of Dollars	
Company	Paid Since	# Yrs Paid	Sales	Market Value
American Express	1870	128	17.5	36.5
AT&T	1881	117	53.2	72.2
Bank of New York	1785	213	38.5	19.5
Bristol-Myers Squibb	1900	98	16.6	88.8
Caterpillar	1914	84	18.8	19.6
Chase Manhattan	1827	171	162.0	45.2
Chevron	1912	86	36.5	57.4
CIGNA	1867	131	19.9	12.0
Colgate-Palmolive	1895	103	9.3	21.9
Du Pont	1904	94	46.0	67.2
Eastman Kodak	1902	96	15.1	22.4
Exxon	1882	116	118.5	160.6
General Electric	1899	99	49.0	220.8
Goodyear Tire & Rubber	1937	61	13.7	9.8
Johnson & Johnson	1905	93	23.1	77.5
Kellogg	1923	75	6.9	18.0
Kimberly-Clark	1935	63	12.9	27.6
Eli Lilly	1885	113	8.5	75.5
Merck	1935	63	23.7	115.9
Minnesota Mining & Mfg	1916	82	15.3	38.6
Mobil	1902	96	70.0	59.8
J.C. Penney	1922	76	29.6	15.7
Pfizer	1901	97	12.5	90.0
Proctor & Gamble	1891	107	35.8	98.6
Sprint	1939	59	15.0	22.4
Texaco	1903	95	47.0	32.2
Walgreen	1933	65	13.4	12.8
Xerox	1930	68	18.1	27.7

THE UNIVERSE OF MUTUAL FUNDS

The universe of mutual funds can be split into two broad groups according to the marketing and distribution method established by the mutual fund company. One group consists of the mutual fund companies which choose to market to, and distribute directly to, investors. The other group includes the fund companies which have chosen to market to, and distribute through, professional financial advisors who in turn will sell the mutual funds to their investor-clients.

Which group is better for the investor? It depends upon who you talk to!

The media refers to these two groups as "No-Load" and "Load" respectively. Load is a term referring to commissions paid by investors in order to invest in the fund. "No-load" mutual funds which market directly to investors have no need to pay commissions to financial advisors because financial advisors are not a part of their marketing and distribution effort. "Load" mutual funds, in contrast, rely primarily on financial advisors in their marketing and distribution effort and they compensate the financial advisors for the service by paying them commissions for selling their mutual funds to investors.

NO LOAD, NO HELP

The professional advisors refer to these two groups as "No Help" and "Help" respectively. The advisors say that investors who purchase no-load mutual funds do so without the benefit of a professional financial advisor's help. You must know what you are doing and you must know what you want before investing in the no-load mutual fund, for when you call the 800 telephone number what you get is a friendly order-taker who is not in the business of offering investment advice. He will take your order for brochures and prospectuses and see that you get them in the mail. He will take your phone orders and follow any instructions you give him regarding your account. You will never hear from him again. You are on your own regarding all of the financial decisions you must make.

Every time you dial that 800 number, you will not talk to the same person twice. The anonymous person on the other end of the telephone knows nothing at all about you: nothing about your other investments and investment experience, nothing about your tolerance for risk, nothing about your income, your net worth, your tax bracket, your financial resources, your financial goals or your time frame for achieving them. The 800 telephone number is simply a method for do-it-yourself investors to request information for analysis and self-study, and/or to provide investment instructions to the mutual fund company.

LOAD = HELP

The professional advisor refers to load mutual funds as "Help" funds because the commission is paid to secure the professional help of the advisor. This help comes in the form of face-to-face personal consultations, one-on-one education, and a comprehensive financial planning process during which the advisor learns all that she can about you and your goals, resources, experience and personal financial situation in order to advise you on a suitable strategy and make specific recommendations, all of which are custom-tailored for you. There is an ongoing, long-lasting professional relationship as your advisor monitors the results of that strategy over time through periodic portfolio reviews. Your advisor keeps abreast of changes in the world of investing, and changes in your life, either of which may necessitate adjustments in your investment strategy.

WHICH IS BETTER?

The financial media often touts the fact that an investor who pays a 5.75% commission on a $1,000 investment is only getting a $942.50 investment, and will publish charts and performance records showing how the $1,000 will grow so much bigger than a $942.50 investment. In essence the media is implying that: 1) the $57.50 commission is not worth the value a professional advisor brings to the table, and 2) no-load mutual funds will outperform load mutual funds due to the commission-less advantage. The media promotes the position that the do-it-yourself investor will fare much better on her own using no-load mutual funds than paying a commission to an advisor and investing in load mutual funds.

The professional financial advisor will point out the fact that the media receives billions of dollars in advertising revenues from no-load mutual funds. Since no-load mutual funds market directly to investors, the way they reach them is through full-color, full-page advertisements in the financial media. This instills some loyalty, if not obligation, on the part of the financial media to propagate the idea that no-load mutual funds are the best way to go. The professional financial advisor will invite the client to peruse the latest issue of his favorite, supposedly impartial and objective financial magazine and count all the references made to specific no-load mutual funds, and compare these to the number of references made to specific load mutual funds. The client is often quite surprised to discover just how heavily weighted the focus is on the no-load funds.

WHICH IS BETTER *FOR YOU*?

Which is better for you: load or no-load mutual funds? It depends upon how you would answer these questions: Do you want help with making your financial and investment decisions, or do you want to do it entirely on your own? Do you feel you have all the education and experience you need in order to make your decisions on your own? Do you have the time, and the interest, in conducting your own research and monitoring the performance of your investments over time? Would you find value in engaging the services of a professional financial advisor - someone with education, training, and experience who is in the business of helping people make such decisions - to help you with your decisions?

Note that not all professional financial advisors offer load mutual funds to the complete exclusion of no-load mutual funds. There are other ways to compensate professional financial advisors besides paying commissions. You will learn all about professional financial advisors in the next three chapters. Whether or not you pay a commission to invest in a mutual fund may not be as important as some people believe it to be.

EVERYBODY PAYS TO GET INTO IN MUTUAL FUNDS

Ignore the anti-commission argument. The truth is, one way or another, every investor pays to get into a mutual fund. It may not come right out of your pocket, off the top of your investment dollar as in the up-front commission example above. But it comes from somewhere. Every mutual fund must pay the marketing and distribution costs associated with getting the word out to potential investors in order to attract its investors. They may pay the newspapers and magazines for all of the advertising they must do, or they may pay professional advisors commissions instead.

Either way, they pay. And when we say "they" pay, it really means the investors pay.

When it doesn't come directly from the investor's initial investment in the form of a commission, it comes out of the operating expenses of the mutual fund company. This affects the return on investment the investor will receive just as much as if it was deducted up front in the form of a commission. How could it not have any effect? If the fund did not have to pay anything for advertising, the fund would have that much more money in it and each share in the fund would be worth that much more. This may be a simple illustration but it nonetheless makes the point that every investor shares in the expense of marketing and distributing her mutual fund whether that fund is a load or no-load fund.

In terms of investment return, do the no-load funds outperform the load funds? This is not the right question to ask. It's like asking: do the blue cars outperform the white cars? The question you should ask is this: in terms of investment returns, would you fare better on your own or with the help of a professional financial advisor? You will find excellent mutual funds in which to invest, including long-term top-performers, among all the major mutual fund families regardless of whether they are no-load or load funds. Take any mutual fund in existence and 99% of the time you will find one that outperformed it over some period of time.

There are thousands of mutual funds available, both load and no-load. The ones that will do the best job for you will do the best job not because they are load or no-load but because they are suitable for you in terms of your particular financial goals, your existing investments, your investment experience, your time horizon, your tolerance for risk, etc.

MUTUAL FUND OPERATING EXPENSES

Every mutual fund company is a business and just like other businesses it has ongoing expenses which are classified into three categories. All mutual funds, whether load or no-load, have

Management fees, 12b-1 Plan of Distribution Fees and all the other expenses related to running a business including salaries, computers, telephones, and administration which are grouped together as Other Expenses.

Management fees are paid to the professional portfolio managers and research analysts who choose the specific investments for the mutual fund portfolios: what to buy, what to sell, and when to buy and sell them. The 12b-1 Plan of Distribution Fees pertain to the selling expenses associated with marketing and distributing the mutual funds, including advertising and "Dealer Concessions" (these are the commissions and service fees paid to financial advisors for selling and servicing the funds).

All three categories taken together are called Total Fund Operating Expenses and they are expressed as a percentage of Average Net Assets, and they are expressed in dollar terms (how much you would expect to pay in expenses on a hypothetical investment of $1,000 over different holding periods). This enables you to compare the expenses of one mutual fund against another.

Some businesses are run more efficiently than others, and so it is with mutual funds. Total Operating Expenses directly impact the bottom line in any business, including mutual funds where it affects investment returns. Everything else being equal, a mutual fund with lower operating expenses should be expected to outperform an equivalent mutual fund with higher operating expenses.

SALES COMMISSIONS AND DIFFERENT CLASSES OF SHARES

This discussion pertains to the advisor-distributed mutual funds which involve commissions. There are often different classes of shares available for investment within the same mutual fund. The difference between the classes relates to the costs an investor will bear, either directly (out-of-pocket) or indirectly (because they are part of the fund's operating expenses) to buy or sell shares in the fund. Although each class of shares is priced independently of the others, and the investment returns are calculated separately, it is usually the same mutual fund managed by the same portfolio managers.

CLASS A SHARES

As in our example above, if the commission is 5.75% and you're investing $1,000, the mutual fund deducts $57.50 from your $1,000 for the commission and the net $942.50 is the amount that is actually invested in the fund. The fund retains a small part of the commission and passes along the bulk of it to the broker-dealer firm which in turn splits it with the professional advisor who sold the fund to the investor. The mutual fund shares sold in this manner are called Class A shares.

The Class A share commission rate may be reduced once you reach a certain level of assets with the mutual fund company. The more money you invest with a particular fund family, the lower the commission rate you may pay. The different levels are called breakpoints, and they may kick in at $25,000, $50,000, $100,000, etc. Each new breakpoint has a new, lower commission rate than the previous level. To help you qualify for a breakpoint the mutual fund companies may aggregate all of your holdings from all of the specific funds in which you're invested in that family of funds, including past purchases. If those earlier investments have grown in value, they will use the newer higher value in the calculation. If you agree to invest within the next thirteen months a certain amount which is equivalent to one of the breakpoints, and you sign a Letter of Intent, they will charge you the lower rate in advance of your commitment (or assess the proper rate afterward if your commitment fails to materialize).

CLASS B SHARES

The mutual fund companies created a second class of shares which are called Class B shares. These are designed especially for investors who like the idea of having a professional financial advisor helping them but who also have an aversion to paying an up-front out-of-pocket commission to pay them. With these, you do not pay any commission up-front so the $1,000 you put in is fully invested. However, should you sell your shares within a certain period of time after purchasing them, the fund will charge you a commission based upon the sale amount. This is called a Contingent Deferred Sales Charge (CDSC), labeled "back-end load" by the media.

The actual commission amount is contingent upon when you sell your shares, and is computing according to a schedule of rates which decline over time. Not all fund families have the exact same schedule, but here is a typical schedule: if you sell within the first year of purchase you may pay a 6% commission; 5% in year two, 4% in year 3, 3% in years 4 or 5, 2% in year 6, and 1% in year 7. After the 7th year passes the CDSC disappears and you will not be assessed any sales charge at any point beyond the 7th year. Keep in mind that the applicable percentage is computed upon the amount of the sale at the time of the sale, and not on the amount of your original investment. If your original $1,000 investment grows to $1,575 and you liquidate in full in year 3 of our example, you will pay a sales commission of 4% of $1,575. The sales commission ($63) will be deducted from the gross amount of the sale ($1,575) and the mutual fund company will send you a check for the net proceeds ($1,512).

Continuing with the same example, if with your original $1,000 investment you purchased Class A shares with a 5.75% sales commission, you would have paid $57.50 and had the difference of $942.50 invested in the fund. With Class B shares, your full $1,000 was invested up front, but by selling in year 4 you paid a

$63 sales commission, which is actually 6.3% of your original $1,000 investment. You can see that although Class B shares charge no up-front commission, they can be more expensive if you are not able to hold the investment beyond the 7 years it takes for the CDSC to disappear.

With Class B shares your advisor will still be paid a commission by the mutual fund company even though it does not come out of your own pocket up-front. Like the no-load mutual funds, the Class B mutual fund will take the money out of the operating expenses of the company to pay the commission to the advisor who sold the fund. Some investors will pay the CDSC for selling out before the commission schedule expires and some investors will never pay it because they will hold their shares long after the schedule expires. Whatever the mutual fund collects in the way of CDSC money, it keeps in order to offset operating expenses. It does not pay these out to advisors, because the advisor was already paid up-front.

CLASS C SHARES

A relatively new class of shares has emerged recently. With Class C shares, the investor may pay a 1% commission up-front, and some fund families charge nothing at all up front. There may also be a CDSC of 1% on the back-end which stays in effect for the first 12 or 18 months of ownership, after which it disappears altogether. Again, some fund families may not charge this CDSC either.

The main feature of Class C shares is that the fund company will pay the advisor who services the fund .75% to 1% a year each and every year the investor holds the fund. The investor will not pay this service charge out-of-pocket, but this money will come out of the operating expenses of the fund which, as always, will affect the investment returns of the fund.

This class of shares is designed to appeal to investors who like the idea of having a financial advisor but who do not want to much in the way of commissions either up-front or on the back-end. This class of shares is designed especially to appeal to advisors who like the idea of working under a fee-based asset management arrangement since the advisors on the Class C shares are paid annually for the service they provide.

OTHER ITEMS WORTH NOTING

Some fund families do not offer Class B shares or Class C shares. Other fund families may use different terminology to distinguish its offerings, Class I and Class II for example. The fund and/or your advisor will help you understand the differences and specific details. The fund's prospectus puts it all in writing for you.

In addition to all of the above, virtually every mutual fund company which chooses to market and distribute their funds through professional financial advisors will also pay an annual .25% service fee to the brokerage firms to help them offset the ongoing administrative expense of servicing the accounts, which the firms share with their advisors. This amounts to 25 cents for every $100 in invested assets, and it comes out of the operating expenses of the mutual fund company. When advisors sell mutual funds to their clients they become the first, and sometimes only, point of contact for the client. The client always has the option of calling an 800 number and dealing directly with the mutual fund company, but many clients prefer to rely entirely on their advisors for all of their information and servicing needs.

WHICH CLASS OF SHARES IS BETTER FOR YOU?

It's as much a personal preference as it is a performance question. Are you willing to pay as much as a 5.75% commission for the services of your financial advisor *once, up-front* and be done with it (as in Class A shares)? Or would you prefer to "finance" it *over time* (as in Class B and C shares)? The "financing" with Class B shares eventually terminates (almost always after seven or eight years), but with Class C shares it continues for as long as you own the investment.

The only way to accurately answer the performance question is to compare all three classes of shares *for the same mutual fund* side by side *for the same period of time*. As usual, the longer the period of time for the comparison, the better. Herein lies the problem. Class B shares as a group have not been around nearly as long as Class A shares (and Class C shares have been around for even less time). In most cases there isn't sufficient data to make an adequate comparison.

Until actual performance data accumulates, the best you can hope to do is to make an educated guess. Generally speaking, the shorter the time frame, the greater the influence an up-front commission will have on investment performance. The longer the time horizon, the lesser the influence that same commission will have on performance.

There is no question that 12b-1 fees also impact performance. If these fees disappear after seven or eight years, as in the case of Class B shares, the longer the time horizon, (beyond the seven or eight years they are assessed), the lesser the influence they will have on performance. If these fees never disappear, as in the case of Class C shares, the longer the time frame, the greater the influence they will have on performance.

This may be seem confusing to you (and understandably so!). Suffice it say that in terms of growing capital over the course of a lifetime, you are likely to do just as well with either Class A or Class B shares, and over the course of a lifetime you could reasonably expect Class C shares to underperform Class A and Class B shares.

PROPRIETARY FUNDS

Many of the large national brokerage firms have their own "in-house" mutual funds. They are proprietary because the only way you can invest in them is through a registered representative of the firm. The firms selling these funds caught some flack when it was discovered that they offered their advisors higher commissions for selling the firm's own funds over all others. Most if not all of the firms proclaim to have discontinued this practice. If your advisor is recommending his firm's proprietary mutual funds don't be afraid to ask about his commission structure and/or if he is receiving any additional compensation or other incentives for recommending them over any of the other non-proprietary alternatives.

Commission issues aside, you should think carefully about investing in a brokerage firm's in-house funds. There are other considerations which may surface long afterward.

If you recall, a typical financial advisor may end up at four or more brokerage firms over the course of his career, and most of his clients will follow him wherever he goes. If he is your representative of record on your non-proprietary mutual fund accounts, all you need to do is sign a "Change of Representative and/or Broker-Dealer" form authorizing the mutual fund company to reregister your advisor as your official representative of record at his new brokerage firm. It is a standard industry practice and this universal form is widely accepted by virtually every mutual fund family - with the exception of the proprietary funds of the major brokerage firms.

If your mutual fund accounts are proprietary, the only representative of record the firm will allow is another advisor at the *same* firm, which is fine if you plan on staying with the firm. If your advisor leaves that firm and you want to go with him to his new firm, you must first sell your proprietary mutual funds and reinvest the proceeds elsewhere. This may cost you money in the form of commissions: you may have to pay a Contingent Deferred Sales Charge on the sale, and/or you may have to pay new commissions when you reinvest the proceeds in new funds. In addition, if you held the proprietary funds in a non-qualified retirement account, the sale will also have taxable consequences which may cost you money. All of these issues are avoidable by avoiding proprietary funds.

Even so, some of the proprietary funds have actually performed quite well over relatively long periods of time, and they may be worthy of your consideration in either of these situations: the account in which you intend to hold the proprietary funds is a qualified retirement account, or you are a long-time faithful client of the firm and do not plan on leaving the firm even if your advisor does.

HOW MUTUAL FUND SHARE PRICES ARE CALCULATED

The Net Asset Value per share is the price of a share in a mutual fund at a given point in time. At the end of every business day the mutual fund will add up all of its assets (all of the investments it owns in its portfolio), and subtract all of its liabilities (all the expenses it owes) to get the Net Asset Value for the fund. Then it divides this by all of the shares owned by investors in the fund to derive the Net Asset Value per share (NAV). If you place an order to buy or to sell shares during the course of the day, the mutual fund must wait until the end of the day when it calculates the NAV in order to know and give you the most current price for your transaction.

Another relevant price is the fund's offering price, also known as Purchase Offering Price (POP). In the case of direct-distributed (no-load) mutual funds the POP is the exact same price as the NAV. In the case of the Class A shares of advisor-distributed (load) mutual funds the POP is higher than the NAV because it includes the amount of commission which will be paid and deducted when purchasing each share in the fund. The POP and NAV of Class B shares will also be the same because no commission is deducted from the offering price.

Virtually every major mutual fund's NAV is published daily in virtually every major newspaper in the country, so it's easy to keep track of them. Some people make the mistake of thinking that an NAV of $10 is somehow better than one at $43 (perhaps because it's perceived as cheaper). This is a mistake because the price is simply a function of the formula used to calculate it. The higher-priced share may simply be a much larger fund with a much larger portfolio of investments which may or may not be better than a smaller fund. The portfolio may have a large asset value or hold higher-priced shares of company stocks but this does not automatically translate into a better-performing portfolio. Or perhaps the higher-priced fund may have fewer investors and fewer shares outstanding so when it divides the fund's NAV by the smaller number of shares it gets a higher price per share, which may or not be better than the lower-priced fund.

HOW MUTUAL FUND INVESTMENT RETURNS ARE CALCULATED

The better way to compare one mutual fund against another is not by price per share but by performance. You want to know how well that share price has grown over time. A good part of the investment return is determined by how well the managers have chosen the investments in the portfolio. If they grow in value so will your corresponding price per share. If you paid $40 a share at the start of the year and it was worth $44 at the end of the year, your investment grew by 10% that year. If you paid $10 at the start and it was worth $8 at the end, your investment lost 20% of its value.

Also included in the calculation of investment returns is all of the earnings of that fund, which may consist of dividend income, interest income, and capital gains. Because the fund holds shares of stock of companies which pay dividends, and/or bonds which pay interest, the fund will regularly receive this money from these companies. They must pass the dividend and interest income through to the fund's own shareholders, according to the percentage of ownership each shareholder owns in the fund (i.e. pro rata).

Likewise, throughout the year the portfolio managers are buying and selling investments for the portfolio. If they sold an investment for more than they paid, they'll have a gain. If they sold an investment for more than they paid, they'll take a loss. At least once a year they have to add up all of those trades and derive a net gain or loss. They must pass along the gain, pro rata, to the fund's shareholders. This is called a capital gains distribution.

Investment return is determined by how well the portfolio managers mange the portfolio with everything considered: the declared investment objectives of the portfolio, the specific investments they selected for the portfolio, when they bought and sold them and the prices they paid and received, the dividends and/or interest income they received, how they respond to current and forecasted economic and market conditions, all of the expenses incurred in the management of the portfolio, etc. All of these things are reflected in NAV, and when NAV is tracked over time we determine the actual investment return of an investment in that mutual fund for given periods of time.

Information on all mutual funds is widely available, including especially investment returns. You can get it directly from the mutual funds (which must meet strict legal requirements in their reporting of information to the public), and you can get it from a wide variety of external sources (newspapers, magazines, businesses which monitor and publish mutual funds' performance records).

You can easily determine a mutual fund's performance for the year-to-date as well as its historical performance for the one, three, five, ten, fifteen, twenty years or whatever period of time it has been in existence. These are most often presented on an *average annual return* basis, where they essentially add up all of the returns for all of the years being measured and divide by the number of years being measured.

WHY MUTUAL FUND INVESTMENT RETURNS ARE CALCULATED

Everybody wants to know where the best place is to invest their money. They want to find the best mutual funds they can find in order to help them get as rich as they can as fast as they can. The most common way people search for the best mutual funds is by evaluating the investment returns of mutual funds and comparing them against each other. The most common way is not necessarily the best way. The investment returns are an important ingredient in the formula, but they are not the only ingredient. You want performance, but you also want consistency in that performance. You want long-term performance.

One mistake many people make is to focus on short-term performance records. The media promotes this short-term outlook every time it publishes the investment returns of mutual funds because all of the attention is on the year-to-date, latest year, three-year and five-year performance numbers. Lots of people chase after last year's top-performers, but last year's top performers are often not this year's top performers. This means that these people not only missed last year's top-performers but by moving money around they are likely to miss this year's top performers as well!

The performance number in which you should be most interested is the average annual return for the period of time most closely aligned with your own investment horizon. As we said before, if you are investing in common stocks via the mutual funds which invest in common stocks, you should have a time horizon of *at least* five years. As a "Millionaire in the Making", your investment horizon is substantially longer than five years. If you are a long-term investor with twenty years of investing before you, wouldn't you be interested in knowing how a fund has performed over the last twenty years? If the fund hasn't been around for twenty years, then look at the average annual returns for the longest period of time they are available.

It matters less that a fund was the top-performing fund in the world last year if it fails miserably in comparison to others for the last twenty years. How does the fund (and your money) hold up during down markets? It may take at least a ten-year track record to get the best idea of how skilled the managers are at managing money in different types of economic and market conditions.

Another thing to remember when comparing investment returns among mutual funds is to be sure you are comparing apples to apples and oranges to oranges. You should not be comparing the performance of a mutual fund that primarily invests in small companies to a fund that primarily invests in large, blue chip companies, or to a fund that invests in high-grade bonds of a foreign government or to a fund that invests in lower-quality bond of American companies. You should only compare mutual funds with similar investment objectives. Only compare mutual funds investing in small companies with other mutual funds that invest in small companies, and only compare funds investing in blue chips with other funds investing blue chips.

And speaking of the managers, how much experience do they have? How long have been at the helm of the particular fund in which you are contemplating investing? The prospectus of a mutual fund will tell you who is managing the fund, how long they have been managing it, and what other experience they have. Funds which change managers are not as predictable: different managers have different ideas about how to run the fund, which affects the investments they will hold in the portfolio, which affects the investment returns of the fund. The mutual fund performance records are most valid when the same people have been consistently responsible for producing them, which also makes them a better indicator of possible future performance.

Always remember that past performance is never a guarantee for the future, but the longer the performance and the more consistent that performance, through good times and bad, the more confident you should feel in your effort to achieve that consistent performance going forward.

READ THE PROSPECTUS

Before you ever consider investing money in a mutual fund be sure you read and understand the prospectus, which you can get directly from the mutual fund company (and often from your professional financial advisor as well). A separate prospectus exists for every mutual fund in existence, and they are often updated annually so make sure yours is no more than one year old. A mutual fund company is legally required to publish a prospectus and to furnish every prospective investor with a copy of it.

The prospectus is often accompanied by (often wrapped by) a colorful, glossy, albeit truthful, marketing piece about the fund, but there is nothing colorful or glossy about the prospectus itself! The prospectus is a legal document which details everything you need to know about the mutual fund. As such many of them were not written in investor-friendly language, but in "legalese" which made for some very dry reading. Things got so bad that the Securities and Exchange Commission (SEC), the federal agency which regulates the securities industry including mutual funds, discovered that people were not reading the prospectuses. As a result, the SEC now allows mutual fund companies to present the most important information in abbreviated form, using concise language written in "plain English," with the declaration that a prospective investor can always get the full legal version (often called the Statement of Additional Information, upon request at any time).

The most important information will be found in all prospectuses. You will learn all about the fund's financial results for the last ten years (if it has ten years of history), and how it measures and derives these numbers. You will learn what the fund's investment objective is, what the fund invests in, and how it attempts to achieve its investment objective. You will learn how the fund is managed, who manages the fund and how long they've managed it, and what fees and expenses are involved in managing the portfolio and administering the fund. You will learn how the fund is structured as an organization, and how it fits into the mutual fund company's larger organization.

If the fund offers more than one class of shares, you will learn all about the differences between them, including commissions involved. You will learn how to buy, sell, and exchange shares of the fund. You will learn how the fund determines the value of its shares, and how to obtain regular updates on share prices. You will learn about your options regarding fund distributions (dividends and capital gains) and their related tax implications. You will learn about other shareholder services available to you, and how to contact the fund.

The prospectus is a gold mine of information. Take advantage of it. Read the prospectus!

You will find excellent mutual funds in which to invest, including long-term top-performers, among all the major mutual fund families regardless of whether they are no-load or load funds.

The truth is, one way or another, every investor pays to get into a mutual fund.

The question you should ask is this: in terms of investment returns, would you fare better on your own or with the help of a professional financial advisor?

One mistake many people make is to focus on short-term performance records. Lots of people chase after last year's top-performers, but last year's top performers are often not this year's top performers.

Take any mutual fund in existence and 99% of the time you will find one that outperformed it over some period of time.

You want performance, but you also want consistency in that performance. You want long-term performance.

If you are a long-term investor with twenty years of investing before you, wouldn't you be interested in knowing how a fund has performed over the last twenty years?

The prospectus is a legal document which details everything you need to know about a mutual fund. Before you ever consider investing money in a mutual fund be sure you read and understand the prospectus, which you can get directly from the mutual fund company.

SHOULD YOU USE A PROFESSIONAL ADVISOR?

In a word: Yes!

My bias is obvious in that I am a professional advisor. But I didn't start out as one. I started out as a do-it-yourself investor, and I made many of the same mistakes the typical do-it-yourself beginning investor makes. Mistakes cost money. The more I learned about investing the more I wanted to learn, and I learned so much that somewhere along the line I decided I wanted to help others learn too, to help them prosper financially, and I evolved into the professional advisor I am today.

And I continue to learn. The world of investing is continually evolving, constantly changing. It is important to stay abreast of the changes and the latest developments because they have the potential to affect you financially, for better or for worse. Lack of knowledge can cost you money! And this is the first argument I would make in favor of using a professional advisor.

A professional advisor may help you increase your investment results. A company called DALBAR, Inc. conducted a twelve-year study (from 1984 through 1996) of investments made in more than 5,000 mutual funds. It determined that investors who used a financial consultant outperformed those who didn't by more than 16% in their equity fund investments and by approximately 31% in their fixed income fund investments.

DO-IT-YOURSELF INVESTORS OFTEN GET DO-IT-YOURSELF RESULTS

Why? Investing can be very emotional. Beginning investors are especially emotional due to their inexperience, and due to their inexperience they make mistakes which cost them money. For example, a typical beginning investor who decides to invest in mutual funds will look at a fund which had the best track record last year and put his money there, not understanding that last year's top performer is rarely this year's top performer. Peter Lynch, the legendary portfolio manager of the Fidelity Magellan fund from 1977-1990 and one of the biggest advocates for the individual investor wrote in *Working Women* in June 1993: "Buying last year's biggest winner is foolish." Yet many novice do-it-yourself investors do just that.

Another common mistake made by the beginning investor is to panic the first time his investment drops in value, and sell the investment at a short-term loss instead of holding on for the longer-haul growth. This is understandable - who can bear to watch the value of your hard-earned capital decline in value? - but it is nonetheless a serious mistake which is extremely detrimental to long-term wealthbuilding.

A professional advisor takes the emotion out of investing, and becomes the objective, rational, well-trained, experienced consultant he or she chose to be. A professional will take the time to learn all about you: to determine where you are right now and where you want to go, and then help you get there. He'll know your tax situation, your tolerance for risk, your time horizon for each of your goals. He'll tell you how much you'll need to invest to reach your goals, he'll help you choose the specific investments that are right for you, but he'll always work within your budget because he wants to see you succeed with your saving and investing program right from the start.

Perhaps best of all, a professional advisor will educate you, face-to-face, one-on-one, as part of the service he provides. A professional advisor helps you stay the course, for the long haul. He'll hold your hand if that's what you want or need, not only at the beginning but also through the choppy waters and roller-coaster rides we all experience as investors. A professional advisor can be worth his or her weight in gold.

There are more than 8,000 mutual funds out there. How on earth do you know which ones are right for you? How many individual funds do you need? How do you best allocate your investment dollars? In other words, of the amount you have available for investing, how much should go into which type of fund to achieve the best possible results for you? Do you have a retirement plan through work? How does this fit into the big picture of your life?

This book answers these questions, but only in general terms. This book knows absolutely nothing about you personally and cannot possibly begin to custom-tailor a strategy that's just right for you.

GETTING ADVICE FROM WELL-MEANING FRIENDS

You probably have friends who are more educated about investing than you are, and they are eager to share with you the benefit of their wisdom and the depth of their experience by offering specific advice regarding your personal situation (whether the advice was solicited and invited, or not). The advice may come from someone you like and trust, and best of all it is free.

Sometimes the advice you receive from friends is accurate and helpful. Often, however, the advice you receive is incomplete at best and just plain wrong at worst. Acting on such advice could be detrimental to your financial health and well-being.

If you had a friend who spent hours poring over medical journals and texts down at the library as a hobby, would you choose her over a doctor to perform surgery on you? Would you trust an unlicensed contractor to do electrical, plumbing or construction work for you, especially if the work involved the safety and well-being of your family? What makes it any different to entrust your hard-earned money to the advice of an untrained, unlicensed friend?

Your friend may indeed be more knowledgeable than you and can help you, so use him as a resource and sounding board, but be wary of acting solely upon the advice of your friend. Tempting as it may be to act upon the free financial advice of our self-educated, well-intentioned friends, beware that it is simply not the same as consulting with a professional financial advisor. The friend may be self-educated and have hands-on experience with his own portfolio, but he has not received the professional training and does not have the full-time commitment and experience necessary to manage money on behalf of others. A friend's advice may appear to be free, but if incorrect or incomplete information causes you to miss out on opportunities or worse, to actually lose money, then the "free" advice becomes costly. Your financial future is at stake. Why take chances with it?

GETTING ADVICE FROM MAGAZINES

Many people read financial magazines for information. Again, this is fine for a general education, but you won't get professional attention, custom-tailored, personal service out of magazines any more than you can get it out of a book or from well-meaning friends.

The majority of articles published in newspapers and magazines are written by professional journalists, not professional financial advisors! The purpose of the articles is to attract more readers and sell more newspapers and magazines, which in turn will increase advertising revenues for the publishers. Granted, the articles will not attract readers unless they offer value, and professional journalists are well-trained to conduct careful research and present it well, and they do provide value. But professional journalists are educated and experienced in journalism, and they have no education or experience in managing money professionally for clients. Professional financial advisors do have this formal training and hands-on experience advising people face-to-face, one-on-one, where every client's personal situation is different.

You can find list after list of mutual funds and their performance histories published regularly in newspapers and magazines. They'll rank mutual funds in order of performance and they may even tell you which specific ones you should own. You may also notice that these lists are never the same from one publication to the next, or even from one month to the next in the same magazine! How could they possibly sell any magazines if the information wasn't changed from month to month, and wasn't presented differently than the competitors' information? And don't forget to ignore the "fear and greed" headlines which are also used to sell magazines. Bypass the emotional appeal and go for the meat of the articles which don't insult your intelligence.

For the most part, I do respect and appreciate the financial media and I hope you find the newspapers and magazines helpful in terms of the general education you will receive by reading them and staying current on all the latest investment trends. But I also hope that you will never invest money in a mutual fund based solely on the recommendation of a three-dollar magazine, will you? The magazine gets thrown in the trash: don't throw your money in after it! When it comes to actually investing your hard-earned money, a professional journalist is no substitute for a professional financial consultant.

THE PROFESSIONAL DIFFERENCE

Professional financial advisors not only have the professional training, full-time commitment, and hands-on experience managing money for others, but they also have a wide array of professional resources available to them which the average investor does not have. The professional advisor is plugged into the industry and constantly receives information regarding the economy, the markets, investment products, and the profession.

There are continuing education requirements to meet, which ensures the professional advisor stays abreast of the constant changes in the profession. The professional advisor belongs to trade associations, and regularly attends conferences, meetings, and presentations offered by these associations and by investment company sponsors, where she also mingles and networks with her colleagues and peers to share ideas and information.

The advisor receives constant communications from the investment company sponsors (including mutual fund companies and insurance companies) from mailings to phone calls to personal visits by representatives of the mutual fund and insurance companies. The company representatives have a direct connection to the movers and shakers at the company, including current perspectives and outlooks about the economy and investment markets, and how they intend to strategically respond to these forecasts. Many fund companies regularly arrange for financial advisors to participate in conference calls with the portfolio managers themselves to get the information straight from the people responsible for managing all the money.

THEY DO IT ALL FOR *YOU*

Remember, the professional advisor will take the time to understand *your* goals, assess *your* current situation including *your* present resources and accomplishments to date, evaluate suitable alternatives for *you*, propose a customized strategy with specific investment recommendations designed to assist *you* in achieving *your* goals, (whatever those goals may be), help *you* implement that strategy, and help *you* monitor *your* results over time, making any necessary adjustments to accommodate the changing conditions in the investment world and the changing conditions in *your* life.

Again, this book provides you with the general knowledge and, hopefully, the motivation and belief you can succeed, to enable you to become a millionaire through saving and investing part of all you earn, but it is not a substitute (because there is no substitute) for the face-to-face, personal, custom-tailored strategy and ongoing financial advice that can be obtained from an educated, experienced, friendly, caring, professional advisor.

A twelve-year study of investments made in more than 5,000 mutual funds determined that investors who used a financial consultant outperformed those who didn't, by more than 16% in their equity fund investments, and by approximately 31% in their fixed income fund investments.

There is no substitute for the face-to-face, personal, custom-tailored strategy and ongoing financial advice that can be obtained from an educated, experienced, friendly, caring, professional advisor.

HOW TO FIND A PROFESSIONAL ADVISOR

The best way to find a professional financial advisor is through the referral and recommendation of a trusted acquaintance who has had personal experience with the advisor. If the advisor is doing a good job, people are more than happy to refer family and friends to the same advisor.

The advisor should honor the commitment that all client-advisor relationships are confidential. You should feel comfortable referring people to the advisor knowing your advisor will not discuss your personal financial situation with others.

Financial advisors come from many different backgrounds and are found in many different settings. Some are stockbrokers. Some are life insurance agents. Some are tax preparers. Some are part of a financial planning firm. Some are employees of their firms. Some are self-employed independent financial planning practitioners who own their own practices. They may be sole proprietors and sole practitioners, or in partnership or incorporated with others.

Stockbrokers are licensed by the National Association of Securities Dealers (NASD) after passing an NASD-administered securities exam. Stockbrokers, who are officially known as Registered Representatives, must always be registered as a representative of a securities brokerage firm. They may be an employee of the firm, or an independent contractor with the firm. Regardless of their compensation arrangement, the brokerage firm assumes regulatory and supervisory responsibility for the stockbroker.

Insurance agents must be licensed. There is no national exam or license registry: each state has its own registration and licensing requirements. California, for example, administers a licensing exam, issues insurance licenses, and regulates insurance agents. An agent may be an employee of an insurance company or insurance agency, or may be an independent contractor who is appointed by one or more insurance companies to transact business on their behalf.

Unlike stockbrokers and insurance agents, anybody can call himself a financial planner, financial advisor, or financial consultant. You need more information than the title someone puts on his business cards. Never hesitate to ask a prospective advisor to describe his or her education, training, experience, licenses, professional affiliations, employment and compensation arrangements.

Although some of the specific *activities* performed by financial planners, like providing investment advice or selling securities or insurance, are regulated by federal and state government agencies, no federal agency and only some states regulate financial planners. In the absence of uniform governmental regulation, the financial planning profession itself sought a way to protect the public through self-regulation. Out of this effort emerged the Certified Financial Planner (CFP)® designation, which is now one of the most widely-recognized and highly-regarded designations in the financial planning profession.

CERTIFIED FINANCIAL PLANNERS

The CFP designation was first introduced in 1972 as a means to reassure the public that those financial planners who are CFP licensees have voluntarily agreed to adhere to high standards of competence and ethical practice. CFP® and CERTIFIED FINANCIAL PLANNER® are federally registered marks of the Certified Financial Planner Board of Standards (the CFP Board). The CFP Board is a non-profit independent professional regulatory organization that owns the CFP marks and authorizes their use by licensing only those individuals who meet its strict certification requirements.

Candidates for CFP licensing must demonstrate they have completed a college-level curriculum in personal financial planning. They must then pass a 10-hour, two-day exam which tests their knowledge of the components of financial planning. They must document work experience which includes financial planning-related experience. And lastly, perhaps most importantly, they must agree to adhere to and abide by a strict standard of professional conduct as detailed in the CFP Board's *Code of Ethics and Professional Responsibility.* In addition, all CFP licensees must regularly fulfill the CFP Board's continuing education requirements and comply with its ethical standards.

The CFP mark is so well-regarded that financial planners have been found to lie about it, claiming they are licensed to use the Certified Financial Planner mark when in fact they are not. The CFP Board legally prosecutes these people when the abuse is discovered. You may call the CFP Board toll-free at (888) 237-6275 to confirm a CFP licensee is in good standing. You may also use the same toll-free number to lodge a complaint against an actual CFP licensee.

The CFP Board investigates consumer complaints, imposes disciplinary sanctions as warranted, and shares information with other regulatory bodies. The CFP Board may suspend or revoke a licensee's right to use the CFP marks if it finds that the licensee has violated the *Code of Ethics and Professional Responsibility.* It's important to note that the CFP Board does not and cannot regulate everyone who calls themselves a financial planner. The CFP Board can only regulate those financial planners to whom it licenses the use of the Certified Financial Planner (CFP) marks.

You will find good, competent, honest, and ethical financial advisors in every setting, but the Certified Financial Planner mark is a mark of distinction. My bias is obvious in that I am licensed to use the Certified Financial Planner mark. I also obviously believe that those financial planners who are dedicated enough to the profession to invest the time, energy, and money necessary to obtain and retain the CFP designation by meeting the strict certification requirements demonstrate a professional commitment that sets themselves apart from the rest of the pack.

The public seems to agree. In 1995 the CFP Board of Standards conducted a survey of 500 households with $50,000 or more in annual income. It discovered that 64% of people whose last consultation with a CFP professional reported being "very satisfied" compared to only 49% of those who last consulted with a non-certified planner. In addition, 56% of those surveyed strongly agreed that "If I wanted to retain the services of a financial planner, I would insist he or she be certified."

Are there bad Certified Financial Planners? There are good and bad people in every profession and trade, including those who break the professional trust placed in them, whether they break it willfully or unintentionally. You can find good, mediocre, and bad auto mechanics, plumbers, carpenters, doctors, lawyers, and accountants. The same holds true for financial planners, including Certified Financial Planners.

Also, financial planning is a very personal business, so personality naturally plays a role. You may have a positive experience with an advisor, and proudly refer a friend to the advisor only to discover your friend didn't quite hit it off with the advisor as well as you did.

A personal referral is an excellent starting point for finding an advisor, but you may want to ask around and get more than one recommendation. Interview three or more financial planners, through free initial consultations, until you find one you like and trust. Liking the advisor means you get along well together, perhaps even become friends. Trusting the advisor means you are confident the advisor is putting your interests first. It is more important to trust an advisor than to like her, but it makes a big difference if you like her too. Then stay with him or her for as long as the relationship is mutually rewarding. Loyalty is highly valued in any relationship.

By the way, advisors tend to move around a bit. A typical stockbroker will have affiliated with four different brokerage firms over the course of his career. Most clients move right along with their trusted advisor. After all, they are "married" more to their advisor than to the firm he happens to be registered with at any given time. These moves involve lots of paperwork: every firm has its own "New Account" forms which must be completed by every client for every account, and additionally there is a "Change of Representative and/or Broker/Dealer" form which must be completed anytime such a change occurs. If you choose to follow your advisor you'll have to help him satisfy the paperwork requirements. It's inconvenient but it's a small price to pay to keep your advisor.

Once you do eventually find your advisor, share with him or her your goal of becoming a millionaire (and feel free to mention you are using this book as your handbook). Your advisor will embrace your goal with joy and enthusiasm (in the unlikely event this isn't your experience, find another advisor immediately).

You will want to know how financial advisors are paid, which is the subject of the next chapter.

The best way to find a professional financial advisor is through the referral and recommendation of a trusted acquaintance who has had personal experience with the advisor.

Never hesitate to ask a prospective advisor to describe his or her education, training, experience, licenses, professional affiliations, employment and compensation arrangements.

HOW FINANCIAL ADVISORS ARE PAID

Advisors are paid by their clients in the following ways:

Commissions. Many investments (including common stocks, mutual funds, and insurance) are sold with commissions paid to the financial advisors who sell the investment. The commission structure varies, depending upon the product being sold. Sometimes you pay the commission up front, off the top, out of your own pocket, and sometimes you do not. If not, the advisor will still be paid a commission but it comes from the operating expenses of the investment company. (You'll learn more about mutual fund commissions in the next chapter).

The advisor must be a licensed, registered representative with a securities brokerage firm in order to receive commissions for securities-related transactions (stocks, bonds, mutual funds). If your state government requires it, the advisor must be licensed as life insurance agent and appointed by the insurance company in order to be paid commissions for insurance transactions (life, health, disability).

You never pay commissions directly to the advisor, but rather to the sponsor of the investment product, which keeps some of the money for itself and passes along the remainder to the advisor. In securities-related transactions the brokerage firm also keeps some of the commission before passing along the remainder to the registered representative.

Hourly Fees. Advisors may charge an hourly fee for their advisory services. You engage and pay the advisor by the hour, and phone consultations may be billed at the same rate as office visits. In earlier times, when the financial planning industry was just getting started, many planners would charge a lump sum flat fee to prepare a comprehensive written financial plan. You may still find some advisors who prefer to work on a fee-for-project basis where they charge a single flat fee to review your situation and make recommendations, instead of charging by the hour. Hourly fees will vary from advisor to advisor, and may vary depending upon the nature and scope of the service requested and provided.

Asset Management Fees. The advisor may instead work under a fee-based asset management plan, where he charges an annual fee that is a predetermined percentage of the assets he is managing for you. If you have a $50,000 investment portfolio, for example, and the fee is 2% a year, you pay the advisor $1,000 a year . The fee is typically paid in quarterly installments which are deducted directly from your account. There is frequently a minimum account size requirement for fee-based asset management.

You will pay this management fee year in and year out. If your hypothetical $50,000 account grows to $75,000, the 2% fee grows with it, and you'll pay $1,500 to the advisor (presumably giving the advisor incentive to continually growing your portfolio).

The fee-based percentages are likely to be structured on a sliding scale according to the size of the account. You may be charged 2% for accounts less than $100,000, 1.5% for accounts between $100,000 and $250,000, and .75% for anything larger. This is just an example - the actual numbers will vary from firm to firm. Always do the math to translate the percentages into the actual dollars you will pay.

The annual fee is in lieu of commissions. You should not be paying any commissions, transaction charges, or any other fees for transactions within the managed account. Also within the managed account you should have available to you a wide array of mutual funds from a number of different mutual fund families. The asset management plan will typically group all of your managed investments into a single brokerage account and you will receive a single, consolidated statement of your holdings on a regular basis.

Combination of Commissions and Fees. Some advisors may charge hourly fees or retainer fees, and accept commissions too, perhaps even from the same client. More likely, they may be compensated by commission with one client, and have a fee arrangement with another client. Fee-based asset management accounts, however, should always be free of commissions.

THE PROS AND CONS OF THE VARIOUS COMPENSATION METHODS

Commissions. Any time there is a commission involved in a transaction, you can pose the question: "am I being sold this product because it is the right product for me, or because it is the right product for the salesperson"? It might be the "right" product for the salesperson because the commission they are being paid for the product they are offering you is higher than the commission on an alternative product. It's an excellent question to ponder, and unfortunately only you can answer it for yourself based on the research and analysis you conduct beyond the salesperson's selling efforts and/or on how much you trust the salesperson.

We have all had negative experiences with salespeople to whom we paid a commission. We have also had positive experiences with truly professional salespeople who took the time to understand our needs (perhaps even helping us become aware of needs we didn't know we had), educated us on various alternatives available to meet our needs, recommended one or more of the alternatives, guided us through the buying decision, and followed up to ensure our continued satisfaction beyond the sale. We paid a commission to that salesperson, and we paid it with pleasure because we ended up with the right product for us, perfectly suited to our needs, and we received outstanding service throughout the process.

Commissions have been the predominant method of compensating financial advisors since the birth of the profession, and they remain so today. As a result, the financial services industry attracts two types of people. There are professional salespeople who have selected financial services as their chosen field for selling, and there are people who are dedicated to their work and to the financial services profession who also happen to be compensated primarily by sales commissions. When they are doing it right, aren't these two types one and the same?

Doing it right means doing the right thing for people, providing outstanding service with honesty and integrity, putting clients' interests before your own, matching their needs with just the right products for them. When the professionals are doing it right, you'd never know the difference between the professional salesperson and the professional financial advisor who chooses to be compensated by commissions because both are serving with the same commitment and dedication.

It is relatively easy to enter the financial services profession, but it is very difficult to survive in it. It is a financially rewarding profession for those who do survive. But just like investing itself, the truly great rewards do not happen overnight, they happen over time. If the advisor continues to do the right thing for enough people, word gets around, referrals will come and the clientele builds. Until then, it is often a struggle for the advisor to make ends meet. It is when the pressure is on to produce that advisors are most tempted to compromise their commitment to put clients' interests before their own.

When it comes to mutual fund commissions, the commissions are well-defined by the mutual fund families and they are paid uniformly. This means that the commission you pay to invest in a particular fund is the same regardless of who sells it to you. You will pay the same commission if you buy that particular fund through an advisor employed by a national brokerage firm, from an independent financial planner, or directly from the mutual fund family itself. The fund families themselves establish the commission rates, and these may vary from fund family to fund family, but whatever the rate is, it is the same for everybody.

If your advisor offers you an investment that cannot be offered by another advisor at a different firm, a red flag should automatically go up that forces you to conduct more research into the reasons, (including especially the advisor's commission arrangement), why that particular investment is being offered over a more universally available alternative. Additionally, if your advisor is pressuring you in any way to make a quick decision, leave and do not return. Long-term investors must always make decisions, but never under the pressure of the moment.

Financial planning is time-consuming. The advisor must take time to get to know the client, analyze the client's situation, evaluate and recommend alternatives, implement the selected alternatives, and monitor the results over time. The commission is only paid if, and when, you agree with your advisor's recommendations and you purchase the recommended investments through your advisor. There is nothing wrong with paying a commission to your advisor for purchasing a recommended investment as long as you are secure in the knowledge that the particular investment is right for you, which happens naturally when you are secure in the knowledge that your advisor is the right one for you.

Advisors lament that the fact that we think nothing of tipping a waiter or waitress 15% or more every time we go out for a meal, yet some people balk at paying a 5.75% commission to a financial advisor for help with some of the most important decisions of their lives. Recent research indicates that people who have invested in mutual funds involving a commission tend to hold their investments longer than those who purchase the "no-load" funds. We might surmise that the reason is they are less likely to sell out for the wrong reasons, thanks to the continuing guidance of their professional advisor who advises them not to panic and sell in a market decline, or not to sell their existing fund in order to free up the money to chase the latest top-performer. Perhaps it is simply because they paid a commission to get into the fund and they're going to "get their money's worth" by sticking with it over time. Either way, if you are avoiding costly mistakes and improving your results, paying a commission to an advisor might be considered an investment in itself rather than an expense.

If you believe your advisor is the type of individual who puts your needs before her own, who invests the time necessary to do a good job throughout the entire financial planning process, who is committed to helping you succeed financially, who is, in other words, someone you trust, you should have no issue with paying a commission to the advisor who helps you implement your investment strategy with the specific investments recommended by your advisor.

You pay your commission up front with the understanding that that advisor is always available beyond the transaction. Especially if you are a long-term investor, that commission pays for itself in no time at all. If you pay 5.75% up front and hold that investment for 6 years, it costs you less than 1% a year of your initial investment to retain the services of your advisor for those 6 years. With each additional passing year, the "annual" fee continues to decline.

Remember, the commission you pay compensates the advisor for the entire financial process, including the ongoing education you receive from your advisor and the monitoring of results over time. Your advisor remains accessible to you and continues serving you long after the commission was paid. And if you ever feel like you are not getting the time and attention you need and deserve, find another advisor - even if it is after you've paid a commission and purchased an investment through that advisor.

Hourly Fees. There are advisors who only charge hourly fees and feel very strongly that this compensation arrangement is the best for the client. The argument they make, and it is an excellent argument indeed, is that there can never be any question about whose interests are being served through the specific recommendations being made by the advisor because the advisor is not receiving any commissions for implementing those recommendations.

One drawback to this method is that there are only so many billable hours available in any given month, and once these are being consistently filled, the only way the advisor can increase his income is by hiring other advisors and retaining some of their billable fees for himself and/or increasing the hourly fees he charges clients. Hiring other advisors diverts time away from serving clients and reallocates it to meeting the demands of running a business. Higher hourly fees involve a more exclusive clientele, because not everybody is willing and able to afford the higher fees. After finally finding an advisor you like and trust, you may find yourself being relegated to a lower-priced advisor or searching for a new advisor altogether.

Incidentally, the actual hourly fee may have little correlation with the competence and experience of the advisor, and no correlation whatsoever with dedication, commitment and integrity. Paying a higher hourly fee does not guarantee you are getting the best advisor for you, nor does paying a lower hourly fee equate to receiving an inferior advisor.

Another drawback to this fee arrangement is that hourly fees do not seem as conducive to building a long-lasting relationship as the other methods of advisor compensation. The "pay as you go" system works well for people who only need help solving a particular problem at a particular juncture in their life, but it does not lend itself to getting to know people very well. It takes time to build a relationship. Working with a client over time, an advisor gets to see the big picture of a client's life, gets to know the client's family, gets to understand a client's goals and learn what truly matters to that client, gets to go through the important changes in a client's life. On an hourly fee system, time is money. It is difficult to spend a lot of quality time with someone when you know the meter is running.

It may be difficult but it is far from impossible to build a long-term relationship with fee-for-service professionals. It works for attorneys, accountants, psychologists, chiropractors, plumbers, and auto mechanics, and it works for financial advisors. Despite the drawbacks the hourly fee arrangement is the method of choice for many advisors and their clients.

Asset Management Fees. There is a growing trend throughout the financial services industry which is moving away from the traditional commission-based compensation toward the fee-based asset management approach.

The commission-based compensation method requires advisors to continually focus on generating transactions which produce commissions whereas an annual fee relieves some of this pressure because it annuitizes the advisor's income stream. With a commission plan, an advisor's paycheck is only as good as her last commission check. With an asset management account the fees keep coming year after year. These annual fees guarantee an income stream for the advisor and they presumably allow the advisor to spend more time working on client portfolios rather than prospecting for commission sales. Of course the advisor will continue to prospect for new business, but the focus shifts more toward gathering long-term assets *to manage* instead of constantly trying to find new money to invest in commissionable products.

By paying an annual fee to your advisor for the assets she manages for you, you presumably have unlimited access to your advisor without regard to the hourly fee meter running and without worrying about any commission issues because the fees are paid in lieu of commissions. In addition, many asset management accounts have at their disposal the entire universe of both load and no-load mutual funds so advisors may choose among the best-performing funds without regard to commissions. Because the fee is based upon assets under management, the higher the value of the assets the higher the fee, so the advisor has a great incentive to grow your assets and earn higher fees for producing results.

When all of your assets are consolidated into the single account, you receive a single statement once a quarter. Not only does your recordkeeping become much simpler, but more importantly it makes it simpler for both and your advisor to review and monitor your whole portfolio at once. Your advisor can easily move things around within your portfolio when the whole portfolio is contained within a single account. He may want to "rebalance" your portfolio for example, when some part of it gets too far behind or too far ahead where he thinks it should be, and he can reallocate parts of your portfolio among a wide choice of different investments to take advantage of changes in the markets.

There are arguments against fee-based asset management. If the account is not a qualified retirement account, portfolio changes involving the sale of investments may have expensive tax consequences. Besides, long-term buy-and-hold investors do not move in and out of their investments and do not try to outguess the markets. They choose quality investments from the start and confidently stick with them for the long haul. Why pay annual fees for asset *management* when all you want is asset *holding*? Advisors receiving annual fees may feel they must show activity within the account in order to justify their fees. They may make unnecessary portfolio changes to "prove" they are actively managing the account.

If you do need to make portfolio changes, you can just as easily move around different investments within a mutual fund family (with the same taxable consequences if applicable), and the large fund families have an incredible array of investment choices within the fund family itself. More and more mutual fund families are consolidating investors' accounts into single quarterly statements so recordkeeping and portfolio monitoring is getting easier outside of asset management accounts.

Perhaps most importantly, in an asset management account you will pay 1% to 2% a year each and every year. Furthermore, as the value of your account grows, this percentage may remain constant but the actual dollar amount of the fees you pay will increase. In contrast, when you pay an up-front 5.75% commission to make an investment, you only pay it one time. And you pay it with the understanding that your advisor will be available to you long after the transaction, providing you unlimited access to your advisor year in and year out. If you are a long-term investor you effectively spread out your fee over many years: the longer you hold your investment, the lower the "annual" fee. And unlike the asset management account, as your commission-paid investment grows in value over time, your fees do not.

Nonetheless, the fee-based asset management approach is growing in popularity among clients and advisors alike. Minimum account size remains a barrier for many clients, but competition is reducing these minimums. Competition in time will also serve to reduce the fees and/or increase the level of service available through these accounts.

WHAT'S THE BEST WAY TO PAY YOUR ADVISOR?

Whatever way your advisor wants to be paid. This answer is not intended to be trite, or worse - arrogant, but purely practical.

The secret is not in trying to determine which compensation method is best and then trying to find an advisor who is willing to be compensated under that method. Rather, the secret is to find the best advisor you can find for yourself, and then pay that advisor under whatever arrangement you both find suitable.

Whatever the compensation method, do not hesitate to compensate your trusted advisor for the professional service you receive over the years. It may well be one of the best investments of your life.

Whether you decide to employ a professional advisor to help you, or you decide to do all of your financial planning on your own, you now have a firm foundation on which to proceed to the next section. It is time to apply all you have learned and begin down your path of becoming a Millionaire.

The secret is not in trying to determine which compensation method is best and then trying to find an advisor who is willing to be compensated under that method. Rather, the secret is to find the best advisor you can find for yourself, and then pay that advisor under whatever arrangement you both find suitable.

Whatever the compensation method, do not hesitate to compensate your trusted advisor for the professional service you receive over the years. It may well be one of the best investments of your life.

Part Four

THE MAKING OF A MILLIONAIRE

THE MAKING OF A MILLIONAIRE

Now it is time to make the Mathematics and the Mechanics of becoming a Millionaire work for YOU.

This is when and where the Secret Formula and Golden Rules for Becoming a Millionaire come alive for YOU, so that YOU will become the millionaire you want to become!

Your money can be your master or your slave, and the choice is entirely yours. To be the master over your money means you take charge and have your money work for you rather than you working for your money. The way you do this is by converting dollars from Earnings into Capital.

Earnings are the result of work. You need Earnings to survive, and to prosper. It's the money you need to pay your bills, to buy the things you want to have, to do the things you want to do. Either you work for your Earnings, or you put your money to work for your Earnings.

When you put your money to work for your earnings, the money is called Capital. Capital comes from your Savings. Capital is what you set aside from your Earnings to Invest and grow and produce Earnings of its own. As it produces Earnings of its own, you no longer have to physically work for those Earnings. Your money is working for those Earnings, instead of you.

The day your Capital can produce all of the Earnings you need to survive is the day you become Financially Independent. You never have to work for Earnings again. Your money does it all for you.

Every dollar you set aside from your work Earnings brings you closer to this goal. Every dollar you convert from your work Earnings to Capital is a dollar you will never have to work for ever again. That dollar goes to work for you immediately, and it goes to work for you forever. It produces more and more Earnings all on its own.

When the money you convert from Earnings into Capital grows into a million dollars, you become a Millionaire. It doesn't happen overnight. It happens over time. It will never happen unless you make the decision to make it happen. You make it happen by converting Earnings into Capital, one dollar at a time.

When the money you convert from Earnings into Capital grows into a million dollars, you become a Millionaire.

THREE MAGIC WORDS THAT WILL HELP YOU BECOME A MILLIONAIRE

These are the three magic words:

Pay Yourself First

Paying Yourself First is the way you convert dollars of Earnings into dollars of Capital.

Paying Yourself First is the another way of expressing the Secret Formula for Becoming a Millionaire.

Paying Yourself First is how you apply the First Golden Rule for Becoming a Millionaire to your own life.

The trouble with the typical savings program is we wait until we pay all of our bills before seeing how much is left over to save. EARN - SPEND = SAVE. In other words, we SPEND first and SAVE what's left over. This is backwards and self-defeating because little if anything is ever left over. There's always a Black Hole which somehow manages to suck up all of our money when we're not paying attention.

Yours, however, is not the *typical* savings program. Yours is a lifelong commitment to becoming a millionaire. You rearrange the formula to read EARN - SAVE = SPEND. You Pay Yourself First by taking your savings right off the top, and then you learn to live on whatever is left over. You spend *only* what is left over after you Pay Yourself First for saving.

You must decide that no bill is more important to you than your millionaire goal!

You must decide that becoming a millionaire takes priority over all other claims on your money!

When you decide that becoming a millionaire is truly your top money priority, then you will have no problem Paying Yourself First.

Paying Yourself First means that as soon as you get paid - the very same day you receive your paycheck - you put your Savings Contract amount into your Savings Fund. Write a check to yourself for this amount, and deposit it at the same time you deposit your paychecks.

Tell yourself over and over that "No claim to my money is more important than becoming financially independent as a millionaire." Affirm "I choose to acknowledge myself as the most important recipient of my earnings, and therefore I Pay Myself First".

Treat this rule like gold. Make this your "millionaire mantra." "I must Pay Myself *First*. I choose to Pay Myself *First*. I Pay Myself *First*."

Paying Yourself First is one of the most important steps you can take on your road to becoming a millionaire. Is becoming a millionaire your top money priority? Will you do what it takes to achieve your goal?

Paying Yourself First is the way you convert dollars of Earnings into dollars of Capital.

Treat this rule like gold. Make this your "millionaire mantra":

"I must Pay Myself *First*.
I choose to Pay Myself *First*.
I Pay Myself *First*."

YOUR BASIC CHOICE

Here's a way to help you save more money toward your goal of becoming a Millionaire. It builds upon the "Pay Yourself First" principle.

Think carefully about every dollar that comes into your possession. With every dollar you receive you are presented with a Basic Choice: to SAVE it or to SPEND it.

If you save it you move one dollar closer to your goal of becoming a Millionaire. If you spend it, it becomes one more dollar you send off into the world. Ask yourself, BEFORE YOU SPEND THAT DOLLAR and send it off into the world, if you truly believe you will receive value in exchange for that dollar you are about to spend. Then ask yourself if this value is greater than the value you will receive when you are financially independent.

Another way to view the Basic Choice is this: with every dollar that comes into your possession you have the choice of using it to further your own goal of becoming financially independent, or using it to further someone else's financial independence.

Think of every dollar you receive in this way. Everybody is clamoring for that dollar of yours. Companies spend enormous sums of money advertising their products and services over and over and over again in an attempt to entice you to part with that dollar of yours. If you do part with that dollar of yours, *they* have succeeded in *their* goal of moving one dollar closer to *their* financial independence, and it is one dollar less that *you* have to apply to *your* own goal of becoming financially independent.

This not about becoming a miser and hoarding every dollar you receive. What good is the life you would have lived if you merely ended up as "the richest man or woman in the cemetery?"

Money *should* be used to enhance the quality of your life. There is nothing wrong with spending money in exchange for the value it provides. You should be grateful you can use your money to pay for your housing, food, clothing, transportation and all the other necessities and non-necessities which contribute to your comfort, enjoyment, and pleasure in life.

There is nothing wrong with furthering the financial independence of another. If a person or a company provides something of value to you, you should have no problem exchanging money for the value you receive, even if it means furthering someone else's financial independence at the expense of your own.

So this is not about fostering thoughts of lack and limitation or nurturing the negative emotions of envy and greed. This is simply about getting you to think carefully about the money that comes into your life. It is your money. What you choose to do with it is entirely up to you.

The Basic Choice is whether to part with a dollar for value you will receive today, or to save that dollar and put it to work for you so you can receive value in the future. In essence, the Basic Choice is between Instant Gratification and Delayed Gratification. It's been said we live in a world where instant gratification isn't quick enough! Surely we can strike a balance between living all-out for today and squirreling away every last dime for the promise of a better tomorrow.

But do get comfortable with the idea that we can all use more help with the delayed gratification side of the scale. It is okay to sacrifice a little pleasure today in exchange for the financial independence of tomorrow. It is okay to say "No" to furthering someone else's financial independence at the expense of your own. It is okay to take that dollar you might normally have spent without giving it a second thought and use it instead to build your nest egg and further your own financial independence.

Not only is it okay, it's required. This is your Basic Choice.

Just be aware from this day forward that for every dollar that comes into your possession you really do have a choice, the choice is entirely yours, and the choice you make determines how long it takes for you to become a Millionaire.

Everybody is clamoring for that dollar of yours.

Your Basic Choice is this: with every dollar that comes into your possession you have the choice of using it to further your own goal of becoming financially independent, or using it to further someone else's financial independence.

In essence, the Basic Choice is between Instant Gratification and Delayed Gratification.

For every dollar that comes into your possession you really do have a choice, the choice is entirely yours, and the choice you make determines how long it takes for you to become a Millionaire.

YOUR FIRST STEP TO BECOMING A MILLIONAIRE

It's time to set your first savings goal.

What is the amount of your take-home paycheck? (Net, after taxes).

Write it down. $____________________________

How much of this can you SAVE from every single paycheck?

Write it down. $____________________________

When can you start Saving this amount?

Write it down. ____________________________

If you did not answer this last question with "Immediately," then return to the previous question and select a lower amount. It doesn't matter how low the amount is, you must be able to start immediately, and you must do it consistently. "Start immediately" means with your very next paycheck. "Consistently" means each and every paycheck from this day forward.

In other words, choose your Savings figure carefully. The dollar figure you write in here must be an amount you can - and will - set aside for SAVINGS from each and every paycheck, paycheck after paycheck, beginning immediately.

You should know what percent of your total compensation you are saving.

Divide the flat amount you are committed to saving by the amount of your gross (before taxes) paycheck, and multiply the result by 100.

Write it down. __________%

If your income varies from period to period, as it might if you derive it from sales commissions or self-employment, then use a percentage of your income as your savings goal instead of a flat dollar amount. No matter what your income is, commit to saving the same percentage every time you get paid.

Whether you are using a flat dollar amount or a fixed percentage, it's better to start with a lower number to "play it safe" than a higher number which might set you up for failure after a couple of paychecks. You can always increase your Savings figure (and you will) over time. So choose an amount that you are absolutely, positively certain you can stick with no matter what for the next three months.

Whether you commit to $25 or $500, 1% or 25%, prove to yourself you can set aside the same amount every time you get paid - and still survive on the remainder - for the next 90 days.

As time goes on you can and should increase the percentage of your income you can save. You might want to consider annual incremental increases. If you're saving $200 a month this year, can you increase it by 10% to $220 next year? Again, only commit to amounts you can save consistently. Do not sabotage your efforts with ambitious but unsustainable goals. Above all, do what you can to avoid sliding backward and dropping below a previous savings level.

The first time you set aside money from your earnings, you begin Building Wealth, and it moves you one day closer toward your ultimate goal of Financial Independence.

The sooner you start, the sooner you arrive.

The first time you set aside money from your earnings, you begin Building Wealth, and it moves you one day closer toward your ultimate goal of Financial Independence.

The sooner you start, the sooner you arrive.

You are now a "Millionaire in the Making."

YOUR MILLIONAIRE CONTRACT

Today is the first day of the rest of my financial life.

From this day forward I am a "Millionaire in the Making".

From this day forward I commit to doing what is necessary to achieve my goal of becoming a millionaire.

I recognize that I build wealth and become financially independent by converting earnings into capital, and I do this by keeping and saving a part of all I that earn.

From this day forward, I Pay Myself First.

From this day forward I commit to saving and investing at least $__________ or __________ % from each and every paycheck, beginning with my very next paycheck.

My savings goal may be increased at any time.

My goal is to become a Millionaire by the age of __________.

Signed ________________________________

Dated ________________________________

I recognize that I build wealth and become financially independent by converting earnings into capital, and I do this by keeping and saving a part of all I that earn.

From this day forward, I Pay Myself First.

From this day forward I commit to saving and investing at least $__________ or __________ % from each and every paycheck, beginning with my very next paycheck.

My goal is to become a Millionaire by the age of __________.

YOUR MILLIONAIRE JOURNAL

Success breeds success. By keeping track of your savings week after week you will appreciate just how quickly your SAVINGS will grow. This fosters self-confidence and will keep you motivated. After three months you will have proved to yourself that you can save the same amount paycheck after paycheck - and you still survived. You may want to increase the amount you're saving - but only if you can do it comfortably and stick with it for another 90 days. Do nothing to sabotage your savings program. The actual amount you are saving from each paycheck is less important than the act of doing it paycheck after paycheck. Use a blank piece of paper and maintain your Millionaire Journal by recording the following information every time you get paid, filling page after page year after year.

DATE (of paycheck)	AMOUNT (of paycheck)	AMOUNT SAVED	NEW SAVINGS BALANCE
____________	____________	____________	____________
____________	____________	____________	____________
____________	____________	____________	____________
____________	____________	____________	____________

The actual amount you are saving from each paycheck is less important than the act of doing it paycheck after paycheck. Success breeds success.

WHERE TO PUT YOUR SAVINGS

Your assignment this week is to find a place to deposit your savings. You should keep your savings in an account that is completely separate from any other accounts you've got going.

This account will be a temporary parking place for your money. You'll never grow your money into a million by keeping it in a savings account at the bank. We will soon discuss where to plant your moneytree seeds, but for now you need a place to store and accumulate your seeds, and this is the purpose of your "Millionaire in the Making" Savings Account.

It may be helpful and convenient to open a second account at the same bank you're running your paychecks through. The same time you deposit your paychecks you simply deposit the checks you write to yourself. Even better, if you have your paychecks direct-deposited into a bank account, talk to the person who processes your payroll at work about direct-depositing a part of your paycheck into a second, separate account.

Ask people you know where they do their banking, and what they like and dislike about their bank. Ask them if they belong to any credit unions, and what it takes to join theirs.

Generally speaking, credit unions tend to offer consumers a better all-around deal than commercial banks, including requiring low minimums for opening and maintaining your account, reducing or eliminating bank-related fees, paying better interest rates on savings, and charging lower interest rates on loans.

Typically you have to qualify as a member before you can open an account at a credit union, but it's pretty easy to do. If you do not belong to an organization or association embraced by a credit union, find someone you know and trust who has a credit union account. You can open a new account together with a minimum deposit. That automatically makes you a credit union member. You can then open a second, separate account - in your name only - into which you'll deposit your savings. Later, you can do whatever you want with the first account, including close it out, without affecting your new individual account.

Armed with your preliminary research, make a list of at least five banks or credit unions in your area, with phone numbers. Call or visit each bank on your list, tell them you need to open a savings account, and ask them the following questions:

What is the amount they require to open an account?

What fees, if any, are involved with the account?

What is the minimum balance required to maintain the account and/or to reduce or avoid the fees? (Minimum balances and account fees are frequently waived if you're direct-depositing from your paycheck).

Do they pay interest on the money in that account?

If so, what is the Annual Percentage Yield (APY)? APY is the standard measure of interest rates that all banks must compute so you can compare one bank against another.

Tell them you're just gathering information for the moment, thank them for their time, and continue down your list. Expand your list if you're not getting the features you want.

Banks are in business to make money, and they perform many fine services for consumers. But the money business is a competitive business and you will be delighted to learn how eager some banks are to earn your business. Some banks, however, don't want to be bothered with small depositors. Some banks actually charge you money to have a Savings Account at their bank! Shop around just as you would for anything else you buy. Do whatever you can to avoid paying fees to a bank for holding and using your money, which is exactly what they do with it.

The objective here is to find an account that is free, and preferably even pays YOU interest. On the other hand, it should be convenient for you, and if that means paying a little for convenience, then so be it. Do what you must do to make it as easy as possible to deposit money right off the top of *every* paycheck.

Even if it's inconvenient, even if it takes a little work, do whatever it takes to set up and maintain an account for your Savings. This is your "Millionaire in the Making" Account, and it is your top money priority. Isn't it?

You'll find a way to make it work best for you.

Won't you?

Do what you must do to make it as easy as possible to deposit money right off the top of *every* paycheck.

Even if it's inconvenient, even if it takes a little work, do whatever it takes to set up and maintain an account for your Savings.

This is your "Millionaire in the Making" Account.

WHAT YOUR SAVINGS ACCOUNT IS NOT

Your savings account is not a vacation fund.

Your savings account is not a Christmas fund.

Your savings account is not a clothing fund.

Your savings account is not a "Big-Ticket" savings fund, where as soon as you build up a tidy sum you go out and spend it on something (car, computer, big-screen TV, etc.) you wouldn't have been able to afford any other way.

Your savings account is not a fund from which to lend money to a friend or family member who is in a jam.

Your savings account is not an emergency reserve to tap into when you have more bills at the end of the month than you have money to pay for them.

Your savings account is not a depression-relief fund, which you tap into just because you're depressed and spending money helps cheer you up.

Your savings account is not an account to be shared with anyone else or used for any other purpose, reason, or excuse.

IT IS YOUR "MILLIONAIRE IN THE MAKING" ACCOUNT

Your savings account is not to be used for *anything* except for Building Wealth for your Financial Independence. Period. There is no target for your money that is more important than this. Right?

You are a "Millionaire in the Making" and this is your "Millionaire in the Making" Account.

Your savings account is not to be used for *<u>anything</u>* except for Building Wealth for your Financial Independence.

You are a "Millionaire in the Making" and this is your "Millionaire in the Making" Account.

THE GREATEST WEALTH-BUILDING SYSTEM IN THE WORLD

Here's a great tool you can use to help you Pay Yourself First. Put your savings program on "auto-pilot". Auto-pilot means it happens automatically. If you've arranged to have your paycheck direct-deposited into a bank checking account, you should also be able to split off a part of each paycheck and direct it into a different, second account which you can earmark specifically for your savings.

If you don't have this option, find another way to make your savings deposit as routine and regular and automatic as possible. Make sure you pay yourself first all of the time - that your savings plan comes first every single time you receive income.

If you struggle with self-discipline like the rest of us, enlist the support of someone you trust to help you stick with your commitment. This person should be someone who understands the value of saving a part of all you earn, someone who will support and encourage you to start your program and stick with it. You might even arrange for this person to check in with you each payday to ask if you've made your savings deposit yet. It's harder to slack off when you know someone's going to be checking up on you.

"Old habits die hard" is a timeless saying which we often associate with bad habits. It applies just as well to good habits. Get into the savings habit. It takes some adjustment at first to take money right off the top of your earnings and put it into savings. Most people do not do this. You are not like most people. You are a "Millionaire in the Making." It's worth the effort and you know it. Once you get started you somehow manage to adjust to having a little less to spend, and before long you don't even miss the money that's going straight into savings. It has become a habit - one of the best habits you can have in this lifetime.

Do everything you can to help yourself stick to your savings program. You're going to have to change the way you're handling your money in order to get into the savings habit, but be assured that once you get your savings program on auto-pilot, you are well on the road to Financial Independence and becoming a Millionaire.

GROWING FROM SAVING TO INVESTING

As you faithfully and consistently apply the First Golden Rule for Becoming a Millionaire: Spend less than you Earn, through your savings program you will soon begin to accumulate some serious money. As you do, you will need to turn your attention to growing your money faster than it can grow in a savings account at the bank. You will accomplish this by investing your money.

This is when you apply the Second Golden Rule for Becoming a Millionaire: Invest your Savings in Appreciating Assets. You can call this your Millionaire Investment Fund, and you will soon learn how to launch it and keep it growing.

But first, a word on the critical importance of having a Cash Reserves Fund.

You are not like most people. You are a "Millionaire in the Making."

Be assured that once you get your savings program on auto-pilot, you are well on the road to Financial Independence and becoming a Millionaire.

THE CASH RESERVES FUND

You know that your Millionaire Investment Fund is not an emergency reserve fund, but this does not mean you should not have an emergency reserve fund. You must have an emergency reserve fund to avoid having to tap into your investments. You never want to tap into your investments, and you most definitely do not want to have to tap into them at the wrong time (when they have declined in value).

Investing in assets which appreciate in value is a long-term strategy. Such assets fluctuate in value on their way toward greater long-term value. You would not want to tap into your investments at one of the times when asset values have declined. You would be forced to sell at a loss. Losing money is detrimental to your wealth-building! It makes becoming a Millionaire take that much longer! Avoid using your long-term assets to meet short-term emergencies.

The solution is to have a separate Cash Reserves Fund (more aptly named because an "emergency" fund or "rainy day" fund almost begs for an emergency and rainy day spending). The Cash Reserve Fund is insurance against any unplanned, unexpected claims against your income. You should keep it in an account separate from your normal operating, bill-paying account. If you choose to also keep it separate from your Millionaire Investment Fund, try to find an account that not only does not cost you any money, but earns you interest.

Your Cash Reserves Fund should consist of all of the income required to meet all of your monthly expenses for at least three months, preferably six months. This could take some time to build up, but you have the time, don't you? And it is when you have a steady income stream that is the best time to fund your Cash Reserves Fund.

You have a choice regarding how to fund your Cash Reserves Fund. You can hold off on your Millionaire Investment Fund until you have completely funded your Cash Reserves Fund to your satisfaction. Since this might take awhile, however, and people are anxious to get started on their Millionaire Investment Fund, they will split their Savings dollars in half. One half of their Savings goes toward building their Cash Reserves Fund and one half goes to their Millionaire Investment Fund.

The choice is yours. The more stable your present income stream the more flexibility you have on funding your accounts. The less stable your present income, the more important it is to completely fund your Cash Reserves Fund as quickly as possible and before getting started on long-term investing. Either way, you must not ignore this step.

Once you have your Cash Reserves Fund established, you can turn your attention, with great excitement and enthusiasm, to your long-term Millionaire Investment Fund.

You know that your Millionaire Investment Fund is not an emergency reserve fund, but this does not mean you should not have an emergency, or Cash Reserves, fund.

Your Cash Reserves Fund should consist of all of the income required to meet all of your monthly expenses for at least three months, preferably six months.

HOW YOU CAN BECOME A MILLIONAIRE

If you have come this far in the book you now know How You Can Become A Millionaire.

Remembering your millionaire mathematics, the objective is to grow your money at 10% a year.

You know that if you invest $264 a month, earning 10% a year, you will become a millionaire in 35 years.

You know that there is no investment in the universe that *guarantees* 10% a year each and every year for 35 years.

You know that you can, nonetheless, achieve a 10% return on an average annual basis if you are willing to assume the risk that your money will decline in value in some years and grow in value in the other years, and that it is through the averaging of the ups and downs that the 10% annual return may be achieved.

You know that common stocks have delivered an average annual return in excess of 10% over the last 70-plus years, and nothing has outperformed common stocks as an investment for this period.

You know that there is no reward without risk. You know that there are ways to manage risk, and they include hiring professionals to help you manage your money, and ensuring your money is diversified in order to reduce, as much as possible, your exposure to any single risk.

You know that mutual funds offer such diversification and professional management. You know that there are mutual funds that invest in common stocks. You know that although there are very few mutual funds with performance records of 70-plus years, you also know that if the mutual funds invest in common stocks and nothing has outperformed common stocks as an investment over the last 70-plus years, you might expect these mutual funds to do as well as the common stocks in which they invest.

You know that mutual funds do have actual performance records themselves. You know that although past performance is never a guarantee for future performance, you also know that the longer the history of a mutual fund, through good markets and bad, the greater the confidence you might have in that particular fund going forward.

Knowing all of these things, you believe you can become a millionaire by investing in common stocks through a mutual fund that invests in common stocks. You hope and expect the mutual fund will deliver to you a 10% return on an average annual basis for the amount you invest over the period of time you choose as your goal for becoming a millionaire.

You know that there are mutual funds that have delivered at least a 10% a year average annual return for twenty, forty, and even sixty-plus years.

All you have to do is look for them, and choose. You can do it on your own, or you can find a professional financial advisor to help you. The time has come to choose, and to act.

You know that if you invest $264 a month, earning 10% a year, you will become a millionaire in 35 years.

The time has come to choose, and to act.

CHOOSING YOUR FIRST MUTUAL FUND

There are thousands of mutual funds available from which to choose. How do you know which one is the right one for you? It is the right one if it meets all of your requirements for your long-term strategy for becoming a Millionaire.

You want a mutual fund that invests in the common stocks of Blue Chip companies. It will state its investment objective as Growth and Income, which it will attempt to achieve by primarily investing in common stocks.

You want a mutual fund with a long-term track record of proven results, in good markets and bad. You recall legendary former mutual fund manager Peter Lynch's opinion that buying last year's biggest winner is foolish. He also said that picking future winners from past performance doesn't seem to work even when you use a three-year or five-year record. (Source: *Working Women*, June 1993). You want your mutual fund to have at least a ten-year track record of delivering an average annual return of 10% or more. The longer the track record, the better. You know that past performance is no guarantee for the future, but the longer the track record the more confident you should feel that the 10% or better average annual return may continue going forward. You can easily find your mutual fund among any one of the largest mutual fund families, as measured by the billions of dollars of assets under the investment management of these companies. Each family has dozens of mutual funds with dozens of different investment objectives. You only need to find a Growth and Income fund with a performance history of ten years or more in which the average annual return (*after* accounting for sales commissions where applicable) is 10% or higher.

Here are the fifteen largest mutual fund families in America, measured by the billions of dollars of assets they have under management, (at this writing), listed in order of their size, with their phone numbers and their primary method of marketing and distribution:

Fidelity Investments	(800) 544-8888	Consumer-Direct
Vanguard	(800) 662-7447	Consumer-Direct
American Funds	(800) 421-4120	Advisor
Putnam	(800) 225-1581	Advisor
Franklin-Templeton	(800) 342-5236	Advisor
T. Rowe Price	(800) 638-5660	Consumer-Direct
Merrill-Lynch	Call local branch	Proprietary/Advisor
American Express/IDS	Call local branch	Proprietary/Advisor
Aim	(800) 347-4246	Advisor
American Century	(800) 345-2021	Consumer-Direct
Janus	(800) 525-3713	Consumer-Direct
Dean Witter	Call local branch	Proprietary/Advisor
Oppenheimer	(800) 525-7048	Advisor
MFS	(800) 637-2929	Advisor
Smith Barney	Call local branch	Proprietary/Advisor

Consumer-Direct means the fund family distributes its funds directly to consumers without the use of advisors and without charging commissions.

Advisor means the fund family distributes primarily through advisors and compensates them accordingly. You may deal directly with these companies but commissions will be charged whether you purchase the funds from an advisor or not.

Proprietary/Advisor means these fund families offer their own proprietary funds through their own advisors. These advisors, however, may also sell any mutual fund from any mutual fund family that uses advisors. You can find an advisor by calling the brokerage firm's branch office closest to you.

Fidelity is unique in that it offers many of its funds directly to consumers without charging commissions, but it also has a number of funds for which it does charge commissions but it does not pay these commissions to advisors. Fidelity does offer a separate class of funds through advisors and it shares the commissions on this separate class of funds with the advisors who sell them.

The above list serves as a great starting point but it's certainly not intended to be an exclusive list. There are many other mutual fund families besides the largest ones listed here, from both the consumer-direct and advisor-distributed categories. You should be able to find a local financial advisor with whom you could meet face to face to learn more about any of the advisor-distributed funds. See the mutual fund chapters and advisor chapters in Part Three of this book for a refresher on these topics.

DO IT NOW

Call the companies in which you are interested and request some general information on the mutual fund family as a whole, including a description of all of the funds in the family. Tell them you are specifically interested in Growth and Income mutual funds which meet your requirements: average annual returns of 10% or better, for 10 years or longer.

Ask for a prospectus and a new account application for these funds, for both a regular account and for an IRA account (which will be further discussed in the *Tax-Advantaged Investing* chapter).

Ask them to include any other consumer brochures they think you might find helpful. The fund companies spend lots of money on producing these brochures. They are designed to promote investing in general, and investing in the fund family in particular, but you will benefit from the exercise so take advantage of the opportunity.

You can make all of these same requests of a financial advisor whether or not you've decided to work with the advisor (it would even be a good test of the quality of service and advice you might expect to receive), and you can do it in lieu of dealing directly with the fund companies or in addition to it.

Start reading through the information as soon as it arrives. Spend time with the prospectus. Some of it may be difficult reading (written by lawyers in "legalese"), but if you go through it section by section you will begin to understand how the fund operates. Compare the prospectuses and brochures of the different funds to learn how they are alike and how they are different.

You want to know what minimum amounts the funds require to open an account, and to make additional investments in the account. Most funds waive these minimums if you agree to allow them to draft a monthly investment automatically from your bank account each month. You want to know what this amount is for each fund you are considering.

As you dig into your research the information may seem overwhelming. Don't let it stop you. Always return to the reason for your research: your mission is solely to find a Growth and Income mutual fund which invests in blue chip companies and which has a ten-year or longer track record of delivering average annual returns of 10% or better. Keep looking until you find one that appears to be just right for you. It shouldn't be too difficult as long as you don't get too sidetracked by all the other information you'll collect. Stick to your mission until it is complete!

Your mission is to find a Growth and Income mutual fund which invests in blue chip companies and which has a ten-year or longer track record of delivering average annual returns of 10% or better.

Stick to your mission until it is complete!

HOW TO OPEN A MUTUAL FUND ACCOUNT

Once you decide on your mutual fund, opening an account is a simple matter of completing a New Account Application and sending it in with your money, similar to opening a bank account.

The New Account Application tells the mutual fund what kind of account you want to open, who you are, and what you want. You provide your name, address, phone number, and social security number. You may include someone else as a co-shareholder, and you tell them how to register the account. You tell them how much money you are enclosing and in which mutual fund you are investing.

You tell them exactly how you want your account to be set up, and you are given an array of different options from which to choose. Some will not apply to you now, and you can ignore them. Some are important to you now, however, so be sure to look for them as follows:

You tell them whether or not you want dividends and capital gains from the fund automatically reinvested back into the fund. You do want this because it is a great wealth-building strategy. Every time the fund distributes dividends and capital gains you buy additional shares of the fund, which really add up over time.

You tell them whether or not you authorize them to accept your instructions by phone (or only by mail, which is slower, more inconvenient, and more expensive than a toll-free phone call).

One of the most important options, however, allows you to set up an Automatic/Systematic Investment Plan. You should strongly consider doing this (see the next chapter for a detailed discussion). If you do choose it, provide the fund with your bank account information and remember to attach a voided check or deposit slip from your bank account.

You must also sign and date the application, attesting to your social security number and acknowledging you have read and agreed to the terms of the prospectus.

If you need help understanding anything, call the mutual fund company and ask for help. If you have an advisor your advisor will help you complete the application. The application for an advisor-distributed fund tells the mutual fund who your advisor is and where she is located. She will receive duplicates of all of your account statements and keep them on file. This allows her to monitor your account and serve as your local contact with the fund. You always have the choice of dealing directly with the mutual fund or with your advisor who acts as your representative with the fund. The fund will acknowledge your advisor as your personally-appointed representative and will take instructions from her on your behalf.

You will receive a statement of your account on a regular basis, usually quarterly, directly from the mutual fund company. Also, anytime there is any activity and/or change in the account the fund is required to send out a confirmation statement, and you will receive one of these every time you make a purchase, every time the fund makes a dividend and capital gains distribution, any time you change your address, etc.

Every statement will tell you how to make additional investments, and will most likely include a remittance slip with your mutual fund account number on it. Even when you send in your money for these additional investments with a remittance slip, write your mutual fund account number on your checks.

Your quarterly statements should also reflect all of this activity for the latest quarter, and the final statement of the year should be an annual statement which details all of your transactions for the year. Once you confirm that all of your transaction details appear on your quarterly account statements, you can discard the interim confirmation statements. If your annual statement has all your transactions for the entire year on it, you can also discard the interim quarterly statements. Keep your records as safe and secure as you do all of your other important papers.

Opening a mutual fund account is a simple matter.

You will receive a regular statement of your account on a regular basis.

Keep your records as safe and secure as you do all of your other important papers.

HOW YOU CAN BECOME A MILLIONAIRE AUTOMATICALLY

You can become a millionaire automatically by investing $264 a month in a mutual fund which delivers an average annual return of 10% or more for thirty-five years. You can and should make it automatic by instructing your mutual fund to withdraw the money you invest each month directly from your savings account at the bank.

The mutual fund company will call it something like Automatic Investment Plan, or Systematic Purchase Plan, and there is a section of the new account application for you to set it up at the time you open your mutual fund account. Mutual funds have minimum amounts they require to open an account and to make additional purchases into the accounts, but most mutual funds waive these minimums when you agree to allow them to draft your bank account for automatic monthly investments. They do have a minimum monthly investment requirement, but these are typically as low as $50 a month (some funds will accept as little as $25 a month!).

You can set this option up after opening your mutual fund account but why not start immediately? You can choose how much you want to invest each month (over and above the minimum), and you can even choose the time of month you want them to draft from your account each month. You can change the monthly investment amount, the drafting dates, and even the bank account from which they are drafted at any time, but give the mutual fund two to three weeks to effect the change.

There are tremendous investing advantages to automatic, systematic investing. It is known as Dollar Cost Averaging and the advantages are discussed in the upcoming chapter *An Investment Strategy for Aspiring Millionaires*. An Automatic Investment Plan is an effective way to Pay Yourself First and it puts your investment program on auto-pilot. Each month automatically brings you closer to your goal of becoming a Millionaire.

An Automatic Investment Plan is an effective way to Pay Yourself First and it puts your investment program on auto-pilot. Each month automatically brings you closer to your goal of becoming a Millionaire!

FEAR AND GREED ARE DANGEROUS TO YOUR WEALTH

We've already seen that fear can immobilize you and prevent you from taking the actions necessary to protect yourself from the Money Monster Inflation, and it can seriously impair your ability to build a lifetime of wealth.

Fear can also cause you take the wrong actions, which may be even more costly than not taking any action. People tend to panic when the market begins one of its unscheduled declines, and sell their holdings at the wrong time: when they've declined in value. Recalling the average bear market numbers from the earlier chapter *When the Stock Market Has a Sale,* can you watch your investment values decline in value 24% (or more) over a period of 8 months (or longer)? Do you have the patience to wait out an additional 13 months (or longer) for a bear market to recover?

Some of these bear markets have taken two to three years to work themselves out. When you're in the midst of a bear market, you have no idea how long the decline will last, how far down the decline will go, or how long it will take to recover from it. Day after day the media fans the flames of fear with bold headlines of gloom and doom.

Have you ever come across a stack of newspapers from the past? Reading the headlines of those newspapers now, you come to the realization that they seemed so important at the time they were produced, but how insignificant and irrelevant they are now. Train yourself to ignore the raging headlines of the moment, the market "disaster de jour," and carry on with your long-term plan of saving and investing a part of all of you earn so you can become financially independent forever. Today's headlines of fear become tomorrow's forgotten trash.

Fear is one of the most powerful human emotions. Fear can make it very difficult to hold your ground and stick to your investment principles when the herd mentality takes hold and the crowd, screaming all the way, rushes out of the store. If you succumb to this fear, you could seriously impair your wealth-building ability and your results. Part of the tremendous value a professional financial advisor brings to the table is to comfort you and reassure you during troubling times, and prevent you from succumbing to fear which can cost you money.

Control your fear! The solution is to view these bear markets as storms in an otherwise pleasant climate. There is no avoiding the storms. They come with the territory. You never know when they will hit. You never know how long they will last. You never know how severe they will be. But you do know they always pass and things will eventually return to normal.

Greed, another powerful human emotion, is on the other end of the spectrum but can be just as devastating to your wealth as fear. Greed develops from a misplaced sense of courage, and it too may be fostered by the short-sighted herd mentality. As market prices go higher and higher and people believe their investment values will continue to increase with no downside and no end in sight, more and more money chases after the highest-returning investments they can find.

As you conducted your research and collected details about the various mutual funds offered by the mutual fund companies you undoubtedly discovered mutual funds with annual returns that greatly exceed your targeted 10% average annual return. You remember your Millionaire Mathematics and understand that the higher the return you can achieve for growing your money, the less time it will take to become a Millionaire. Why "settle" for 10% when you can find funds that have delivered 17% to 22% over the last three to five years? You may be tempted to reach for the highest returns you can possibly achieve, by investing all of your money in mutual funds with the highest annual returns you can find.

This is a mistake which can be very damaging to your wealth. Investment fads change like fashions. Last year's top-performer is typically not also going to be this year's top-performer. The money which chases after last year's top-performer frequently arrives too late and misses the boat. Moreover, that same money may well miss *this* year's top performer by being off this boat when it takes off. In its 1997 year-end review the *Los Angeles Times* advised its 1,360,000 readers "Don't chase performance. It's a loser's game." (Source: *Los Angeles Times*, "Chasing Performance Is a Loser's Game, " January 4, 1998).

Even though Peter Lynch says "Buying last year's biggest winner is foolish," and "Picking future winners from past performance doesn't seem to work even when you use a three-year or five-year record," he went on to say "All this is not to say you shouldn't pick a fund with a good long-term record. But it's better to stick with a steady performer than to move in and out of funds, trying to catch the waves." (Source: *Working Women*, June 1993).

This does not mean that you should settle for mediocre or subpar performance. Some investments *do* deliver consistently higher returns for ten, twenty, thirty years and more, and although they only reveal themselves over time through their proven long-term performance, such funds do exist. These are the steady performers you should find, and stick with, year in and year out.

ARE INDEX FUNDS THE ANSWER?

We often hear how 75% of the professional money managers fail to consistently outperform the market as a whole. Why pay them huge fees to manage our money when we could do better by simply investing in what is known as an Index Fund? In contrast to an actively-managed fund an Index Fund is a "passively" managed fund which is designed to mirror the markets as a whole merely by carefully selecting a basket of stocks intended to serve as a proxy for the whole market and then leaving this portfolio to go up and down as the market will.

Index Funds may outperform some money managers in choppy markets, others in up markets, and still others in down markets, but they do not appear to consistently outperform the same managers under the same conditions. Moreover, the Index typically used in such comparisons has been the S&P 500, which is only appropriate when comparing managers of blue chip stock funds. You cannot use this particular Index as a guide to compare the performance results of managers of bond funds, small company stock funds, international growth funds, etc.

The Indexed Fund then does not consistently outperform the same 75% of professional managers. And even if this were true, it still means that 25% of professionals do consistently outperform the market. These top-performing managers do exist, and so do the mutual funds they manage. Even so, do not get caught up in the game of chasing individual performance returns all over the scoreboard. It is far better to find a mutual fund family of funds whose investment philosophy and money management style is closely aligned with your own. You will find good mutual funds within every family. You do not need to drive a sports car when a safe, reliable, dependable family car will get you where you need to go. The speed limit is the same for all cars. Find the consistent performers and stick with them.

Manage your expectations and do not let your greed run rampant. When the whole stock market experiences two or three consecutive years of returns of 20%-30% or more each year, people begin to expect these returns every year going forward. They may ask themselves and their advisors why they are "only" earning 10% when the market itself is in the 20% to 30% range. They bring in new money to invest and expect to earn 25% on it this year and every year.

Rein in your greed! How can we possibly expect an entire market to appreciate in value 25% a year, year after year? It's not rational! Our Gross National Product (GNP), a measure of our economy as a whole, only grows at 2% to 5% a year. Again, part of the tremendous value you'll receive from a professional financial advisor is to help you manage your expectations by aligning them with reality to avoid making costly mistakes.

ALIGN YOUR EXPECTATIONS WITH REALITY

Common stocks have delivered average annual returns of slightly better than 10% over the last seventy-plus years, and nothing has outperformed common stocks as an investment class. The 1980's and 1990's have proven to be unparalleled in terms of the investment returns experienced by investors in stocks and mutual funds. These returns have been higher than the historical average annual returns measured over the past seventy-plus years. Particularly during the last fifteen years, the market has experienced bursts of rapid appreciation which occur in comparatively short periods of time. These rapid run-ups account for the biggest chunks of the large market gains in any given year, especially in these recent outstanding years.

As more and more people have taken retirement planning into their own hands, through individual investing and through retirement savings plans in the workplace, more and more money has been funneled into the equity markets than ever before in our country's history. Nothing has outperformed common stocks as an investment over the last seventy-plus years, so the long-term retirement money continues to flow into common stocks and into the mutual funds which invest in them. (There are more mutual funds in existence today than there are publicly-traded stocks). One of the basic principles of economics is when demand exceeds supply, prices rise. As more and more money continues to flow into the equity markets, prices rise faster and higher than can be justified by the true underlying fundamental investment values.

As a result, in these same recent times the market has also reached historical levels of overvaluation, which historically correct themselves through “normal” corrections consisting of bear market declines of 15% or more. There have been recent periods, however, when these levels of overvaluation have sustained themselves for longer than usual. Such corrections have been rarer and milder than usual. Bear markets have been completely absent.

Perhaps one day the bottom will drop out and we will experience one sudden, massive no-holds-barred market correction. (Watch the fear run rampant then!) Perhaps this will never happen, and we will instead experience more-frequent but milder “mini” corrections which rotate throughout various sectors of the market one sector at a time, enabling the market to self-adjust incrementally.

What’s an investor to do? How do you strike a balance between reaching for the returns, and assuming the necessary risk required to grow your money in order to become a Millionaire, without succumbing to the powerful emotions of fear or greed, fueled by the herd mentality, which actually drive the markets up and down in the short-term?

The solution is to develop and stick to an investment strategy that will see you through to your long-term goal of becoming a Millionaire regardless of what takes place in the markets on your way to your goal.

Fear and Greed are among the most powerful human emotions, and if you succumb to them they can be devastating to your wealth.

The solution is to develop and stick to an investment strategy that will see you through to your long-term goal of becoming a Millionaire regardless of what takes place in the markets on your way to your goal.

AN INVESTMENT STRATEGY FOR ASPIRING MILLIONAIRES

This investment strategy consists of five parts, each of which is an equally important component of the whole. These separate components have already been identified and emphasized repeatedly throughout the book. Taken together they form a powerful and effective investment strategy for aspiring millionaires. Here they are, in one place.

#1. Have a Long-Term Investment Perspective. This has been the focus of this entire book. Becoming a Millionaire does not happen overnight, it happens over time. When you have a long-term perspective, it doesn't matter what happens in the markets today, this week, or even this year. What matters is what happens over time.

The stock market goes down and the stock market goes up. There is no consistency from year to year, and there are no guarantees for the future.

Fear and Greed may influence the investment markets in the short-term, but it is always fundamental value which drives prices in the long run. If the companies underlying the investments are solid, and their sales and earnings continue to grow, then their value as investments will also grow. Historically, nothing has outperformed common stocks as an investment.

With reward comes risk. You cannot expect returns without assuming the necessary inherent risk. You can try to ignore risk by sticking your head in the sand and "play it safe" by parking all of your money in U.S. Treasuries or Certificates of Deposit at the bank, but you'll be assuming the greatest risk of all to your wealth as the Money Monster Inflation steadily erodes the purchasing power of your money.

IT'S NOT TIMING THE MARKET, IT'S TIME *IN* THE MARKET

Many people play "Hide and Seek" with risk by trying to time the market. They *hide* when they think the markets are too high by pulling their money out, and then they put their money back in to *seek* better returns when they think the markets are priced low enough.

This is called trying to time the market, and it requires an awful lot of guessing. You have to guess at when you think the market is too high, so you can pull out your money before the market falls, (and hope you don't miss out on the market going any higher after you do). Then, if the market does in fact drop, you have to guess at when you think it is has dropped enough so you can put your money back in (and hope it does not keep dropping).

William F. Sharpe, professor of finance at Stanford University found that a market timer would have to be right at least 82% of the time, which is better than 4 out of every 5 guesses, to do as well as an investor who simply bought and held stocks for the same period.

THE PENALTY FOR MISSING THE MARKET

Fear that the market is too high might keep you out of the market, but it can keep you out of the market at the wrong time. Some of the biggest market advances of any given year occur in only a matter of days. If you're out of the market on those days, you will miss those powerful advances which make a big difference in the investment returns.

For the ten years from 1987 through 1996, the stock market (measured by the S&P500, without reinvesting dividends) had an average annual return of 11.8%. If you missed just the ten best days during this ten-year period, you would have had an average annual return of 7.1%. If you missed the best 30 days, your average annual return would have been 1.9%! (Source: American Funds' *Your Retirement Resource*, Summer 1997).

Would you be interested in an investment that produced less than a 2% average annual return for ten years? When it comes to achieving your financial goals, there is more risk being out of the market than being in the market. Missing just the 30 best days out of ten whole years can wipe out all of the advantages of investing in common stocks. Whether it's fear or greed that is motivating you, trying to time the markets is a fool's game. No one can do it successfully and consistently for any length of time.

I live in Huntington Beach, California, where Surf City is our official moniker and where we have many surfers. As any surfer will tell you, the really great waves only come around once in a while. You never know when the next great wave is going to come around, but one thing is for certain: you have to be in the water if you're going to catch and ride the good waves. Investing is a lot like surfing in this respect, isn't it?

WHEN YOU BUY, BUY TO HOLD

Having a long-term perspective means when you buy, you buy to hold. When you make an equity investment, you make it with the understanding that you have become a part-owner of an asset that needs time to appreciate. You are not investing to speculate that your investment will rise rapidly in price so you can sell it for a quick profit, and move on to the next one, and then the next. There are people who attempt to "play" the market by trading stocks in just this fashion. Like trying to time the market itself, trading stocks is a fool's game which will cost you money.

Remember, it is not timing the market, but time in the market, that makes the big difference.

Think of the buy-and-hold long-term perspective as a long distance journey you will be making in your car. You do not get off the freeway and stop at every gas station to buy a gallon of gas to replace the one you just burned up, out of fear you bought the wrong kind of gas or paid too high a price or out of greed that you may be able to get a better brand or better price at the next gas station. You will waste precious time and burn up more money in the constant stopping and going. You're much better off filling up your tank regardless of the price and driving nonstop with the knowledge you will get exactly where you want to go, regardless of what gas prices do along the way.

The same goes for the actual vehicle you are using. You don't need a race car to travel at breakneck speed, and neither do you need a luxury car. All you need is an efficient, comfortable, dependable car that has a proven record of efficiency, reliability, and performance. The speed limit on the freeway is the same for all cars. You do not need to speed (which increases your chances of crashing) and you do not need to impress anybody. All you need to do is find a vehicle you are confident will get you where you want to go in the time frame you have allotted yourself to get there.

Another analogy can be made with gardening. You do not plant seeds and then dig them up the following week to chastise them for not growing fast enough, or pull out the plants to inspect their roots for the same reason. No, you plant your seeds and tend to them with the understanding that they take time to grow. You diversify and plant different kinds of seeds, and you know that they are different plants and they grow at different rates and bloom at different times. In time you know that you will have a beautiful garden full of different varieties of plants and flowers you can admire for years to come.

As a final illustration, take a look at *Forbes Magazine*'s annual listing of the 400 Richest People. You won't find a single market timer or stock trader on the list! The second richest person in

America is the legendary Warren Buffet, who built his incredible wealth as a long-term buy-and-hold investor. Anne Scheiber, whom you met in the *A Word of Encouragement* chapter, also built her fortune as a long-term buy-and-hold investor. As buy-and-hold investors Anne Scheiber became a multi-millionaire, and Warren Buffet a multi-billionaire.

PATIENCE IS A VIRTUE

Patience in life is a virtue. Patience in investing is your one-way ticket to long-term profits, wealth, and prosperity. This is important to remember in the choppy waters, when the markets are volatile and upsetting. This is especially important to remember in bear markets, when your investments are declining in value, spiraling ever downward month after month over the course of a couple of years.

Know that it's also happening to Warren Buffet, as it has happened to Anne Scheiber, and it's happening to every other long-term buy-and-hold investor. They do not panic, they do not sell out of fear. And neither should you. Be patient and know that it's just another bear market, just another sale in the stock market. Remember how you are invested in some of the oldest, biggest, best-managed companies in the world, and they will survive the onslaught the same as they always have.

#2. Stick to Quality. Stick to investments with long histories of proven performance of delivering the results you want. Blue chip stocks have long histories of increasing sales, earnings, and dividends. These are the fundamental, underlying determinants of stock prices.

In the short term, stock prices are driven by *expectations* about the future based upon interpretations about the present. This makes the stock market very emotional in the short term, for it is essentially fear and greed which drive the market in the short term. In the long run, it is *results* which determine value and hence stock prices are based upon results.

There can be no guarantees, but the longer the track record of proven results, the more confident you may feel going forward that the same positive results will manifest themselves in the future. A kid who gets straight "A"s in elementary school will likely continue to get them in middle school, high school, and college. A company which has been a leader in its industry for decades will likely continue to be an industry leader in the years to come.

People like to get excited about Initial Public Offerings (IPOs), privately-held companies which are just going public by selling stock to the general public for the first time. They hear of investors making all kinds of money on these IPOs. Some people do make lots of money, but more often than not the individual investors like you and me do not.

Everybody has an uncle Fred or cousin Margaret who has a "hot tip" on a stock. We are very tempted to put our money into this hot tip, especially after hearing them boast about their past successes. They made a "killing in the market" by picking a stock that "went straight through the roof" right after they bought it. Perhaps they also even sold it at just the right time, right before "the bottom fell out of it." They made a tidy profit, if not a killing. The success stories, and even the hot tips, may occasionally prove to be true winners for them. If you and they, however, continually take this trading approach to heart and invest accordingly, sooner or later you will also end up with a lot of "dogs," underperforming (if not worthless) investments that cost you a lot of money.

Investing is not the same as speculating. We have already learned that there are no stock traders or market timers on the Forbes List of the 400 Richest People. Don't you think that by now, after more than seventy years of stock market investing, if such a strategy were possible, someone somewhere would have risen to great wealth and made the list? Some of the smartest people in the world have searched for and experimented with investing formulas, yet none has ever succeeded consistently.

Warren Buffet became a very wealthy man sticking to quality. When Warren Buffet makes an investment, the whole world knows about it. Take a look at his very public investment portfolio. You will find recognizable, top-quality companies in his portfolio, and you will discover that he bought and held them in his portfolio for years if not decades. Anne Scheiber stuck to quality and invested in blue chip stocks. This is the difference between investing and speculating.

Why gamble with your hard-earned money on unproven IPOs and "hot" stock tips? Especially when there are so very many top-quality companies, and mutual funds which invest in them, all of which have long-term track records of proven performance. Even the stock prices of good companies occasionally go down, but if they are truly quality companies they never stay down. Quality is highly valued. Stick to quality. If this strategy is good enough for the truly "smart money," it's good enough for the rest of us!

#3. Be Well-Diversified. By sticking to quality you stack the odds in your favor, but you have to take it a step further. Even the bluest of blue chips occasionally stumble and fall, and the stock price follows. They generally get back on track and the stock price recovers accordingly, but sometimes it takes a few years. Even with blue chips, do not put all of your eggs in one basket. You must diversify your investment dollars.

Investing in mutual funds provides instant diversification. Where else can $25 or $50 or $264 a month buy you ownership in dozens if not hundreds of some of the largest, best-managed companies in America and in the world? As in the multi-paned window analogy, if one stock in the portfolio should stumble, the dozens of others in the portfolio remain intact and minimize the negative effect of the one.

Of course if the entire market for blue chip stocks declines, the entire mutual fund portfolio follows suit. Although blue chips may temporarily fall out of favor, there may be other classes of stocks which become popular. Small, fast-growing companies may suddenly become fashionable for a while, with investment dollars being funneled into them until the trend changes to something new. Of course when the market for all stocks declines, then small companies and blue chips alike follow suit, just as an ebbing tide lowers all ships. But perhaps the bond market remains intact, so owning bonds or mutual funds that invest in bonds will deliver better investment results than stocks.

The point is, as you build your investment portfolio you can and should diversify among different asset classes through mutual funds which invest in the different asset classes. The better diversified you are, the less impact any one market segment will have on your total portfolio. You will learn more about this in the next chapter.

#4. Invest Systematically. Invest regularly. Put your investment program on auto-pilot. Investing the same amount of money each and every month is one of the best things you can do to achieve your goal of becoming a Millionaire.

This is also known as Dollar-Cost Averaging. By investing the same amount of money each and every month in common stocks, you will accumulate your ownership interest in assets which have historically appreciated in value an average of 10% a year, regardless of what the market is doing in any given month. Market prices fluctuate month after month on its upward climb. Because you're investing a fixed amount at fixed intervals, your dollars buy more shares when prices are low than when they are high. Over the long haul, the average cost of your investments will be lower than their upward-climbing values.

This is a time-tested method of investing which has delivered proven results. The discipline of fixed-amount, fixed-interval investing eliminates the need for trying to time the market and it counter-balances the temptation to succumb to fear and greed.

Over time your fixed-dollar contributions will be even more valuable if you periodically increase the fixed amount of your regular monthly investment.

#5. Use a Professional Advisor. By investing in mutual funds you are automatically relying on the education and experience of professionals by entrusting your money with the managers of the mutual fund portfolios. You will receive a semi-annual report from these managers which details the holdings and past performance of your funds, and this will likely be your only contact with them.

One of the best investments you can make is finding and using a professional financial advisor to advise you personally. Find someone who is competent, ethical, educated and experienced in financial planning. Find someone who will sit down with you face to face, and who will take the time to get to know you and find out what you are trying to accomplish. Find someone who is easily accessible to you, who will take whatever time is necessary to answer all of your questions. Find someone who will spend the time educating you on what you need to know in order to make intelligent decisions. Find someone you like and trust, and with whom you believe you can forge a long-term relationship. Find someone who is committed to helping you achieve your goal of becoming a Millionaire. These professionals do exist, and they exist for you!

<u>#1. Have a Long-Term Investment Perspective.</u> When you have a long-term perspective, it doesn't matter what happens in the stock market today, this week, or even this year. What matters is what happens over time.

<u>#2. Stick to Quality.</u> Stick to investments with long histories of proven performance of delivering the results you want.

<u>#3. Be Well-Diversified.</u> Investing in mutual funds provides instant diversification.

<u>#4. Invest Systematically.</u> Invest regularly. Put your investment program on auto-pilot. Investing the same amount of money each and every month is one of the best things you can do to achieve your goal of becoming a Millionaire.

<u>#5. Use a Professional Advisor.</u> Finding a professional advisor who is committed to helping you achieve your goal of becoming a Millionaire is one of the best investments you can make.

THE PYRAMID PORTFOLIO

Remember the chapter on *The Perfect Investment*? The Perfect Investment is defined as one that would be: free of risk, liquid, protect and preserve your principal, generate income for you, and consistently grow in value each and every year you owned it.

You will also hopefully remember that there is no such thing as The Perfect Investment. It does not exist.

There is, however, a way to obtain nearly all of the features of The Perfect Investment, and that is to construct a *portfolio* of investments in which each investment in the portfolio delivers at least one of the desired benefits of The Perfect Investment. The objective is to have your portfolio in its totality perform as much like The Perfect Investment as possible.

Whether your professional financial advisor helps you, or you choose to do it yourself, portfolio construction and asset allocation play a critical role in long-term wealth-building.

BUILDING A PYRAMID

Constructing a portfolio is much like constructing an investment pyramid, which is built in five layers. The base of the pyramid is the layer called Cash. Investments in this area would consist of checking accounts, savings accounts, and money market mutual funds. You may use this layer to establish and maintain your Cash Reserves Fund as discussed in the earlier chapter. Your Cash Reserves form the foundation of your investment pyramid. The Cash layer contains the "risk-free" and liquid objectives of the Perfect Investment. Liquid means you can get at your cash quickly, if not immediately. Risk-free means you can expect to get what you put in, dollar for dollar at any time, because your principal does not fluctuate in value. Even in a money market mutual fund, although it is never formally guaranteed as it is in a bank account, the mutual fund companies strive to maintain a constant one-dollar-per-share share price.

The layer in the pyramid above Cash is called Income because it consists of investments which generate income as their primary objective. These investments include bank Certificates of Deposit, government bonds, and corporate bonds. The Income layer consists of loanership investments: you agree to lend your money for a predetermined length of time in exchange for receiving regular interest income at a predetermined rate of interest. You expect your principal to be returned to you in full at maturity, when the loan comes due. Before maturity however, your principal will fluctuate in value depending upon what the interest rates for comparable investments are doing at any given point in time (which is important if you have to sell before maturity). The regular income you receive is your reward for assuming the risks involved in lending out your money.

The next three layers in the pyramid are ownership investments in which you exchange your money for an equity position in the investment. Through your ownership interest you share in the risks and rewards of ownership of the assets in which you invest. The layer in the pyramid above Income is called Growth and Income, and it consists of investments which have the dual objectives of growth while also generating income. This is the layer which includes the stocks of Blue Chip companies.

As the companies continue to generate increasing sales and earnings they will grow more valuable over time, and so will your ownership interest in them. This will satisfy the growth objective of the investment. These companies also regularly share part of their earnings directly with their shareholder-owners in the form of dividends. This dividend income will satisfy the income objective of the investment. The total return on your investment in this layer is measured by both the growth in value of your investment as well as all of the dividend income you receive. The dividend income is a large part of the total return, and because the income is regular and serves as an immediate return on your investment, it reduces some of the risk of investing in ownership investments.

The next layer up in the pyramid is called Growth, and growth of capital is its primary objective. This layer consists of companies which are growing faster than Blue Chip companies. Some of these companies will in fact emerge as Blue Chip companies as they mature. In the interim, they pay out very little if anything at all in the way of dividends to shareholders. These companies prefer instead to reinvest their earnings back into themselves to finance their continued growth of sales and earnings, which makes them more valuable as time marches on. Growth investments entail more risk than Growth and Income investments, but they also deliver greater rewards over time.

The final and top layer of the pyramid is labeled Aggressive Growth, and maximum capital appreciation is its investment objective. Here you will find smaller, newer, faster-growing companies. They may be on the cutting edge of their industries (or creating brand new industries) with the newest products and services, meeting the needs of people not currently being met by their larger competitors. They have perhaps found a niche to exploit which their larger competitors may have missed. Virtually all of the Blue Chip companies started as small, new, fast-growing companies which grew larger as they matured.

Compared to larger companies these newer, smaller companies have little history of proven sustainable results. They are however, growing their sales very quickly. They may or may not be consistently profitable. They are, however, perceived to hold great promise. These companies are obviously the riskiest of all investments, but when they succeed, over time they tend to generate the greatest returns on investment than any of the other investment classes.

And so each layer in the pyramid may be considered an investment class, or asset class. As you move up the pyramid, you assume greater risk - in terms of fluctuating market values and possible of loss of principal - in exchange for the potential for greater returns. Moving down the pyramid, you'll forfeit higher returns in exchange for greater stability of principal, but the emphasis placed on safety and stability and preservation of capital brings with it the risk of loss of purchasing power due to the ravages of inflation, which are substantial over time. Within each class there are varying degrees of risk and corresponding opportunities for reward. No matter where you are on the Pyramid, each investment has its own inherent risks. No investment is completely free of risk, which is the only characteristic of the Perfect Investment you will never be able to achieve. All of the other desired characteristics can be found somewhere within the investment pyramid.

ASSET ALLOCATION

To construct a portfolio of investments to model the Perfect Investment, you need to invest some of your money in each part of the investment pyramid. By investing in each asset class you are further diversifying your total portfolio. According to the authors of articles which first appeared in the Financial Analysts Journal in 1986, updated in 1991, more than 90% of a portfolio's total return is determined by the investor's asset allocation policy: what asset classes to hold and in what proportions.

Our attention thus far has been focused on finding and investing in a Growth and Income mutual fund portfolio (investing primarily in Blue Chip stocks, the middle layer of the pyramid) with a long-term track record of average annual returns of 10% or more. Yet we also emphasized you should not even begin investing until you have built your Cash Reserves Fund (the bottom layer of the pyramid). Now we are expanding the discussion to include further diversification by considering investing in the three remaining asset classes: Income, Growth, and Aggressive Growth.

Different investments perform differently under different economic conditions. As you well know by now, by being well-diversified, you reduce the overall risk to your portfolio. In any given year we do not know which particular asset class will outperform the others. The Blue Chips Growth and Income may consistently do well for a year or more. In other years, Aggressive Growth may lead the pack. Growth may be the dominant performer in still other years. And in the years when the equity markets languish, or downright decline in value, bonds in the Income class may outperform stocks, and the steady income from income-producing investments also serves as a stabilizing influence in your portfolio. If you are invested in each asset class, some part of your portfolio should benefit regardless of the economic and market conditions in any given year.

You can find mutual funds in every asset class of the investment pyramid. Although the bottom two layers of the pyramid frequently involve banks (checking accounts, savings accounts, and Certificates of Deposit), you can construct your entire portfolio with mutual funds, providing all of the benefits of mutual fund investing within each layer of the pyramid: diversification, professional management, liquidity, etc.

All of the mutual fund families offer individual mutual funds in each of the asset classes. They have money market funds which are mutual funds which invest in income-producing instruments all of which mature in 270 days or less (and they usually come with check-writing capability in order to provide the same liquidity as a checking account at the bank). There are mutual funds whose primary objective is income and they invest primarily in bonds. We've discussed Growth and Income mutual funds investing primarily in Blue Chips. Other funds strive to achieve greater capital appreciation and they invest accordingly, with either Growth or Aggressive Growth as their declared objective. There are even funds which specialize in investing in a specific sector of the economy, computers and technology for example, or banks, or natural resources. These would be considered Aggressive Growth investments.

One of the most common mistakes investors make is to limit their investments to the first two levels of the pyramid (without even knowing about asset classes and the investment pyramid). Millions of people park their money in savings accounts and Certificates of Deposits in banks around the country. This is perfectly okay if they need a place to temporarily store their money because they need to get at it in the near future, but a lot of long-term money is placed there too. The reason is people perceive the bank to be a safer (less risky) investment than other alternatives. In the short-term this is true. Over the long haul, this is dangerous to their wealth. Market risk (price volatility) is high in the short-term but declines considerably over longer periods of time. Inflation risk, although low in the short-term, increases substantially over time and its detrimental impact on your wealth is great. In your quest for safety you may find that over the long haul your Certificates of Deposit have become Certificates of Depreciation! Loanership investments are the better choice for short-term needs but ownership investments are the better choice for your long-term wealth-building goals.

If you want to grow your capital you need to acquire ownership interests in investments which grow in value over time (appreciating assets). The younger you are and the greater your investment time horizon, the larger the allocation you might make toward the upper half of the pyramid (where your greater returns, because of their inherent risks, will be found over time). In his book The Intelligent Investor, Benjamin Graham, long considered one of the nation's most respected investment authorities, advised even the defensive investor to always have at least 25% of his or her portfolio invested in stocks and 25% invested in bonds. The remaining 50% would be allocated according to your own specific investment needs, goals, and desires. In contrast, the aggressive investor would reduce his or portfolio allocation to bonds and increase the percentage allocated to stocks.

Investors are also realizing the incredible investment opportunities (complete with their own inherent risks) available outside of the United States. "International" mutual funds invest entirely outside the United States while "global" mutual funds invest all over the globe, including the United States. In addition to the opportunities, such international investing allows for greater diversification because the different countries' economies and investment markets perform differently in different years.

HOW TO BUILD *YOUR* PYRAMID

First you concentrate on building your savings in a Cash Reserves Fund to the point of being able to cover all of your monthly expenses for three to six months. Then you turn your attention from saving to investing and launch your Millionaire Investment Fund by investing in Blue Chip stocks through a Growth and Income mutual fund with a long-term track record of 10% or better average annual returns. Then you further diversify by finding and investing in mutual funds among the other asset classes, one at a time. Each fund will have its own minimum requirement for opening an account so you may have to accumulate enough savings to meet this requirement. Alternatively, you can arrange for monthly investments directly from your bank account just as you did for your first fund.

You can usually find all the funds you need within the same fund family, and this has its advantages. Recordkeeping is much easier, especially if you arrange for consolidated statements where all of your holdings are detailed on a single statement. Regular statistics reports from the same fund family makes it easier to track the performance of all of your holdings. Also, if you are paying up-front commissions to invest in your funds through an advisor, you only pay the up-front commission once, enabling you to subsequently transfer money between your various funds commission-free. (Be aware that such transfers involve selling shares of one fund to buy another and the sale may have tax consequences). Additionally, the fund family offers reduced commission rates when your total asset values within the fund family reaches various levels.

Most importantly, you have already done enough initial research to find a fund family you like before investing in your first fund. You presumably made your choice because you like the company's investment philosophy, strategies, and proven performance. Although each fund within the family will have its own separate portfolio managers and corresponding investment results, the fund family's overall approach to managing money will be present within each of its fund offerings.

As you build your pyramid one asset class and one mutual fund at a time, keep in mind that if your overall goal is to grow your money at an average annual rate of return of 10% or better, you must now monitor your whole portfolio to check your progress. When you add a mutual fund investing in bonds for the Income asset class, and the fund has a long-term track of delivering an 8% average annual return, this will tilt your total portfolio's annual return downward from your 10% goal. Likewise, investing in Growth and Aggressive Growth funds with average annual returns exceeding 10% will tilt total portfolio performance upward.

When you conduct your research and dive into performance numbers remember that, tempting as it may be, your objective is not to find the one mutual fund with the highest annual returns so you can put all of your money in it and only it. Greed is dangerous to your wealth. Your objective is to further diversify your portfolio through asset allocation by finding mutual funds among the different asset classes. We never know what any given year will be like in the investment world. You want to supercharge your portfolio with the hope that some part of your portfolio will benefit each year by riding the top-performing asset class wave of the year, and protect your portfolio against sudden downdrafts in any particular asset class.

A SAMPLE ASSET ALLOCATION

In the event you are feeling overwhelmed by the asset allocation discussion, here is a sample allocation you might consider using as a starting point in constructing your own investment pyramid and portfolio. This is obviously a growth-oriented allocation model (70% ownership investments in assets expected to appreciate in value over time), suited for investors with longer-term investment goals and time horizons and tolerance for price volatility.

AGGRESSIVE GROWTH	10%
GROWTH	25%
GROWTH and INCOME	35%
INCOME	20%
CASH RESERVES	10%

This is just a sample allocation. You can and should custom-tailor the allocation according to your own needs and desires. More conservative investors, for example, will allocate less to the top half of the pyramid and more to the bottom half. Your math will be easier to work with if you make your adjustments in 5% increments. Taking 5% away from one asset class means adding 5% to another.

You can even diversify within each asset class. You may, for example, want to split your targeted 20% allocation in the Income category into different types of Income mutual funds, each with its own (different) investment objectives (in terms of how the fund obtains its income). Or you may choose to find a single, diversified Income fund, one which invests in all kinds of income-producing investments, including government bonds, high-quality corporate bonds, and low-quality high-yield bonds, from governments and companies all over the world. They often have names like Diversified Income, Strategic Income, Global Bond, World Income, etc.). Read the prospectuses so you know exactly what you're getting and what's involved in the getting.

INVESTING INTERNATIONALLY

Further diversification can be achieved through international investing. Many of the world's leading corporations are based outside of the United States, including 76 of the world's 100 largest corporations, 8 of the 10 largest banks, 7 of the 10 largest insurance companies, and 6 of the 10 largest broadcasting and publishing companies. More than 70% of the world's stocks are not available in the U.S. stock markets. (Source: American Funds *Capitalizing on a World of Opportunities* brochure, 1997 edition).

There are additional risks involved with international investing, but by diversifying to include investments outside of the United States you can actually improve the results of your total portfolio. Markets around the world move in different directions, which serves not only to reduce the volatility of investment values within your total portfolio but to also position it to capitalize on worldwide opportunities in the emerging global economy. As just one small example, Lucent Technologies informs us that more than half of the world's population has never made a phone call. Free markets continue to open up all over the world, and generating increasing demand for goods and services.

Every mutual fund company offers global and international investing opportunities ("global" means all over the world, including the U.S., whereas "international" means strictly outside of the U.S.). You may want to split your targeted 35% allocation in the Growth and Income category between a domestic Growth and Income fund and an International Growth and Income Fund. You can do the same in the Growth category. Or instead of two funds (one domestic and one international) per category, you may choose a Global Growth and Income fund for the Growth and Income category and a Global Growth fund for the Growth category, and let the portfolio managers make the decisions on where in the world to invest the money.

TOO MANY CHOICES?

How many funds do you actually need in your portfolio? Recent studies indicate that seven or eight mutual funds (assuming the different asset allocation categories) deliver all the diversification you need to construct a completely-diversified portfolio. Anything beyond seven or eight mutual funds delivers only marginal results for the efforts expended.

Don't worry if you don't have enough money to invest in seven or eight funds right off the bat. Keep it simple. Your Cash Reserves Fund and your blue chip common stocks Growth and Income fund is an excellent start. Then expand to fill in the rest of your pyramid, one fund at a time, including global or international investments. Keep in mind that many blue chip companies have a global presence and derive sales and earnings from all over the world. This already gives you international exposure!

Your investment program is a long-term commitment. As time goes on you will accumulate savings to enable you to diversify into other mutual funds. It happens sooner than you think. When you do begin to diversify, tracking your investments gets a little more complicated.

HOW TO COMPUTE EXPECTED PORTFOLIO RETURN

When all you have is one mutual fund in your portfolio, it's easy to compute your expected portfolio return. You simply look at historical average annual returns and expect them to continue. But as you build your portfolio by adding funds from different asset classes, each with different historical returns, how do you know your *whole portfolio* will grow at your targeted growth rate of 10% or more?

By looking at each investment in your portfolio in relation to the whole portfolio, you can calculate what is known as your Expected Portfolio Return. All you need is two numbers for each investment: you need to know the expected return for each investment, and you need to know what percentage of your total portfolio each investment represents.

Look at the sample portfolio in the Expected Portfolio Return chart at the end of the chapter. These are the steps you would take to calculate the Expected (or Actual) Portfolio Return:

First you record the current (or your targeted) value of each fund in the $ column.

Then you add up all of these values to get the Total Portfolio Value.

Then you divide each fund's value by the Total Portfolio Value to determine the percentage, which is called its Weighting (W), that each fund represents in the total portfolio. The percentage is expressed as a decimal, so if the value of the Money Market Fund is 10% of your total portfolio, you record it as .10.

Then you record each fund's Expected Return in the (ER) column. You can use the fund's average annual return (preferably a ten-year or longer average), or you can use the fund's actual return for the past year. Again, percentages are expressed as decimals. The Growth and Income Fund's average annual return of 10.5% is recorded as .105 in the (ER) column.

Then you multiply each fund's Weighting by its Expected Return and record the results (which are carried out to four decimal places in this example) in the last column (W x ER).

Add all of the results and multiply the total by 100 to convert the decimal to a percentage, and this represents your Expected Portfolio Return.

In this example you can expect your total portal to grow at 9.5% a year. If your target is 10.5% you will need to make adjustments. You may want to increase the amounts you are investing in the funds which have higher average annual returns.

This will increase their respective weightings in your total portfolio and raise the Expected Portfolio Return.

You should not, however, transfer *all* of the money in your Money Market Fund and Diversified Income Fund to the Aggressive Growth Fund just because the Aggressive Growth Fund has higher returns. Do not sacrifice diversification in pursuit of higher returns! Leave your current holdings intact. Just commit more of your *future* investment dollars to the higher returning funds until you reach your portfolio target.

It takes a little math but it's worth your time and effort to do the computations. Unless you're making lots of changes (and hopefully you are not), once or twice a year is usually sufficient (certainly no more than quarterly).

How to Calculate Expected Portfolio Return

Fund	$ Value	W Weighting in Total Portfolio	ER Expected Return	Result of W x ER
Money Market Fund	1,200	0.10	0.045	0.0043
Diversified Income Fund	1,800	0.14	0.075	0.0107
Growth & Income Fund	4,500	0.36	0.105	0.0375
Int'l Growth Fund	3,600	0.29	0.090	0.0257
Aggressive Growth Fund	1,500	0.12	0.120	0.0143
Total Portfolio Value	12,600	1.00		0.0925
				x 100
Expected Portfolio Return				**9.25%**

Although The Perfect Investment does not exist, you might construct a *portfolio* of investments to obtain the desired benefits of The Perfect Investment. The objective is to have your portfolio in its totality perform as much like The Perfect Investment as possible.

We never know what any given year will be like in the investment world. By diversifying among different asset classes you hope that *some* part of your portfolio will benefit each year, and you hope to protect your portfolio against sudden downdrafts.

Further diversification can be achieved through international investing. Many of the world's leading corporations are based outside of the United States.

HAVE AN ANNUAL CHECK-UP

In addition to regular physical exams to check your physical health, you should also undergo financial check-ups to check your financial health. Whether you have a financial advisor or are investing on your own, you should conduct a financial check-up at least once a year. An annual portfolio review is necessary to monitor your results and make any necessary adjustments. Pick the same time each year to get into the habit. Your birthday is a good day for this. New Year's Eve is another good one. So is April 15th, tax time.

You should conduct your review using your latest account statements and latest updated average annual returns (performance statistics) from your mutual fund company. Your review should consist of the following:

STEP ONE: Check Your Motivation

Reread and review as much of this book as it takes to keep you fired up about your goal.

STEP TWO: Check Your Savings Progress

Determine the amount of money you made for the year (how much you earned, gross compensation).

Determine the amount of your savings (how much of your earnings you kept and put into savings).

Divide the savings amount by the gross compensation amount (and multiply the result by 100) to determine your Savings Rate percentage.

Does your savings rate percentage meet your approval? Are you converting enough of your earnings into capital so that more and more of your money is working for you instead of you having to work for more and more money?

STEP THREE: Check Your Portfolio Value

Determine the ending value of your total portfolio.

Determine the beginning value (it's the ending value of the previous year).

Subtract the beginning value from the ending value.

Divide this number by the beginning value, and multiply by 100. The result is the percentage increase in value of your portfolio for the year.

The increase in portfolio value will of course be due in part to your regular savings contributions. Look at the cumulative balance of your Millionaire Journal and subtract it from the ending value of your portfolio. The difference is the amount attributed to the growth and earnings of your investments.

You will want to know how the investments in your portfolio are performing.

STEP FOUR: Check Your Investment Results

You can either do it manually or use the published results of the individual mutual funds in which you are invested. To do it manually return to Step Three and compare the beginning and ending portfolio values after subtracting out your savings contributions for the previous and current year. The objective is to compare the growth and earnings in your portfolio from year to year without accounting for the portfolio additions from savings contributions.

Alternatively, determine the average annual returns of each of your mutual funds, updated to include the latest year. You can get these numbers directly from the mutual fund companies. Note: Be sure you are using the same computations every year: if you selected your fund using a ten-year average annual return, keep using a ten-year average to monitor your fund's results (don't use a lifetime average one year, a five-year average the next, a ten-year average the next, etc.).

As the latest year's results are incorporated into the historical average, does the average remain true to your expectations? If you find it slipping downward over the course of two or three years, you should find out why. Based upon the results of your research you may want to re-evaluate your selection.

STEP FIVE: Check Your Asset Allocation Percentages

Group your investments into asset classes. Add up the ending values for each asset class, and divide each sum by the ending value of your total portfolio (multiplying each by 100). This will show you what percentage of your total portfolio is allocated to each asset class.Does this allocation continue to meet your approval? Did any asset class jump ahead or fall behind your targeted allocation percentages? Do you want to reallocate part of your portfolio to bring things into better balance (with possible tax consequences if selling is involved), or just reallocate your savings allocations for the next year?

These questions may be better answered over the course of two or three years. Your portfolio may rebalance itself over several years. One asset class may outperform the others in one year, and an another asset class outperforms the rest in the following year. One or more asset classes may have negative return years. Your whole portfolio may even decline from time to time. Every year will be different, and none can be predicted in advance.

Just remember that you diversify your portfolio because you want to minimize the negative influences and to capture the positive influences, and you never know from year to year what they will be or where in your portfolio they will show up. Monitor your portfolio but do not become obsessed with the perceived need or desire to make constant changes. If you have a millionaire's time horizon of twenty or thirty years, don't fret over one or two years that don't work out as well as you hoped or expected. As long as you keep saving and investing a part of all you earn, and you stick to your overall investment strategy, time will smooth out the temporary bumps, the storms will pass, and you will eventually reach your goal.

APPRECIATE YOUR PROGRESS

You'll be accumulating some serious money before long. Take time on a regular basis to appreciate the progress you are making on your journey toward financial independence.

Think of a way to chart your progress visually. Perhaps you can create a graph and record the total value of your portfolio each year. Or draw a vertical thermometer, much like the kind you see in fundraising drives, with a big bulb at the top representing your goal of a million dollars. Make one hundred tick marks, each representing an incremental $10,000 in value, and fill in the spaces as your wealth builds and you pass each tick mark.

You're on your way to becoming a millionaire! Have some fun watching your portfolio grow!

You should conduct a financial check-up at least once a year. An annual portfolio review is necessary to monitor your results and make any necessary adjustments.

Take time on a regular basis to appreciate the progress you are making on your journey toward financial independence.

Have some fun watching your portfolio grow!

TAX-ADVANTAGED INVESTING

As long as you have a long-term investment horizon you should do everything you can to protect the growth and earnings of your investments from taxation, for as long as you can. Our government encourages us to save and invest for our own retirement because it recognizes the fact that we can no longer count on Social Security and private pension plans to meet our financial needs when we retire. These sources only provide part of what we will need: we are on our own for the rest of it. We must rely largely upon our own accumulated savings to support ourselves. The size of our accumulated nest egg will determine the quality of life we will lead in these later years. The encouragement to save comes by way of tax-advantaged investing which is created and modified by the Congress through the tax laws it passes.

Our retirement years begin when we choose to stop working for our earnings and rely on other sources for the income necessary to support ourselves. With our life expectancies as long as they are, if we retired at age 60 and lived to age 80 we will have had 20 years of retirement. We could easily spend more than a fourth of our lives in retirement. When the money from a job stops coming in, not only do we need alternative sources of income, but those sources of income may have to last 20 years or more. One of the worst things that can happen is that we outlive our income.

Congress has changed the tax laws over the years to induce us to save for retirement, the primary emphasis being the creation of tax-qualified plans which permit tax-advantaged investing. The chief feature of every IRS-qualified retirement plan is that all of the earnings inside these designated plans grow tax-free during all of the years the money remains inside the plan. We are only taxed when we withdraw the money from the tax-qualified plans. The big stipulation is that we must be at least 59-1/2 years old before we begin the withdrawals or face a 10% early-withdrawal penalty on top of the normal income taxes. (There are certain limited circumstances in which the 10% penalty is waived, but they are not pleasant).

In "regular" investing outside of a qualified retirement plan, you must pay taxes on your earnings every year. The bank will send you a 1099 at the end of every year showing how much interest income you received during the year. Mutual funds generating interest income, dividend income, and capital gains distributions will also send you a 1099 every year. Even if you never actually receive the income (because you instructed them to reinvest these earnings back into your fund by buying additional shares), it is as if you did. The IRS calls it constructive receipt.

THE BENEFITS OF TAX-ADVANTAGED INVESTING

Tax-advantaged investing, in contrast, allows you to keep all of your earnings working for you without you ever having to pay taxes on them until you begin to withdraw them. As you might imagine, the positive effect of tax-advantaged investing is substantial, especially over time. As an illustration, if you can earn 9% on an investment, inside the qualified plan you keep all of the 9% return working for you year after year. Outside of the plan, if you are paying 28% in federal income taxes and another 5% in state income taxes on your earnings, this combined 33% effectively reduces your return by one-third each and every year. Instead of earning 9% on your investment, you are effectively earning a third less, or 6%, each and every year.

Doing the math, $264 a month earning 9% a year for 35 years results in an accumulated nest egg of $776,600. The same $264 a month earning 6% for 35 years delivers $376,100. You would still need to pay income taxes on the $776,600 as you withdrew it from the tax-advantaged account, but even if you took all the money in a lump sum and paid the same 33% income tax rate, you still end up with $520,300. This still leaves you with $144,200 more than the pay-as-you-go ordinary taxable accounts.

Another way to make the comparison is to use the Rule of 72 which is a rule of thumb often used to estimate how long it takes to double your money given any rate of return on investment. All you do is divide 72 by your expected rate of return. In our example, 72 divided by a 9% return indicates you will double your money every 8 years. In contrast, 72 divided by a 6% return indicates you will double your money every 12 years. You will obviously double your money much faster inside a tax-advantaged account. If your goal of becoming a millionaire includes living to age 59-1/2 and beyond, you need to explore every tax-advantaged investing alternative available to you.

TAKING ADVANTAGE OF TAX-ADVANTAGED INVESTING OPPORTUNITIES

Start at your workplace. Chances are good that your company has a qualified retirement savings plan in place. In larger companies it may be known as a "401k" plan. In government entities it may be called a "403b" plan, Tax-Sheltered Annuity (TSA), or Tax-Deferred Annuity (TDA). In smaller companies it may be a SIMPLE plan, or a Simplified-Employee Pension (SEP). Other plan designs include Money Purchase Pension Plan, Profit-Sharing Plan, or Paired Plan. Deferred Compensation Plans may or may not be official qualified plans but their intention and operation is often similar to the qualified plans.

The qualified plans allow you to take part of your earnings and set it aside for retirement. This money usually comes right off the top of your gross compensation *before* income taxes are computed and goes directly into the plan, saving you income taxes in addition to helping you save for retirement. Your employer may also match your contributions as further inducement to save. Whether it's fifty cents on the dollar, or a dollar-for-dollar match, think of this as an instant return on your money! The employer may have a vesting schedule which says that the match is 100% yours only if you stay with the company for a certain number of years, and partially yours as you build up to the required number of years of service. Your own contributions remain 100% yours from day one.

Some plans even allow you to borrow from your retirement savings account. Always check with the plan administrator who will always have plan details in writing you can take home and study. Ask your financial advisor to help you interpret the rules and teach you how to use them to your best advantage.

You may often defer up to 15% of your compensation (sometimes up to as much as 25%, depending on the specific plan) up to a predetermined dollar limit. Not only does this save you money on the income taxes you do not pay immediately on the compensation you defer, but everything you defer gets invested and grows free of taxation for all the years it remains in a qualified plan. Add your employer's tax-deferred matching contributions and you can see just how great an opportunity this is. Depending upon your particular situation, your objective could and probably should be to defer the maximum amount possible into a qualified tax plan for as long as possible.

When you leave your employer you have the option to continue the tax-advantaged treatment of your retirement money. Some companies will allow you to leave your money in their existing plan even though you no longer work there. If your new employer also has a retirement savings plan, the new plan may allow you rollover your money from your previous plan to the new one. You always have the right to roll over your qualified retirement plan money into your own Individual Retirement Account, which is often your best choice because your investment alternatives are not limited to the specific offerings of the established plans. On the other hand, you cannot borrow from an IRA whereas you may be able to borrow from a plan at work, but only if the plan itself allows it.

INDIVIDUAL RETIREMENT ACCOUNTS

Once you have maximized the workplace retirement savings opportunity, the next opportunity will be found in the Individual Retirement Account (IRA). Everybody in the country is permitted to contribute $2,000 (if earned income is at least $2,000) a year each and every year through age 70-1/2. Non-working spouses may also contribute $2,000 to their own separate account.

You can open these accounts anywhere you like, including at all the mutual fund families. You can open a new account every year or continue funding the same one(s). You can transfer funds from one IRA to another (called a trustee-to-trustee transfer). You can rollover funds from a qualified retirement plan into an IRA (called an IRA Rollover, and make sure the account is designated as an IRA Rollover). Anytime you move retirement funds, do not take possession of the money yourself. Always arrange for such moves through the plan sponsors and trustees who will also provide the necessary paperwork.

When opening an account you just ask for an IRA application instead of the regular application, and you can choose any of the same mutual funds you always have available to you. The fund company designates the account as an IRA which gives notice to the world (i.e. the IRS) that it is an official retirement account which qualifies for tax-advantaged treatment. This means you will never get a 1099 at the end of any year because all of the earnings within the account grow tax-deferred. Because the account is earmarked for retirement, the 10% early-withdrawal penalty rules apply.

Unlike some workplace retirement plans, you cannot take out a loan from your IRA. Effective in 1998 you can, however, use penalty-free IRA money to pay for some college expenses as well as up to $10,000 for a first-time home purchase.

You can fund your IRA right up until you file your income tax return each year, but the best time to make your contribution is the first day of each new calendar year. This gives you an entire year of tax-deferred growth. If this isn't possible, then keep in mind you can fund your IRA through systematic investing right out of your savings account the same amount each month ($2,000 divided by 12 months is $167.66 a month. Do not exceed the maximum allowable $2,000 per year). Rollovers and transfers do not count as contributions.

Depending upon your Adjusted Gross Income (AGI) each year, and whether or not you have a qualified retirement plan available to you through your employer, you may or may not be able to deduct some or all of your IRA contributions. By deducting the contributions from your reported income you effectively reduce the amount of income on which you are taxed. Many people stopped making IRA contributions because they found themselves unable to take the income tax deduction. This is unfortunate. The deductibility is a nice benefit but the primary benefit of the IRA is the tax-deferral of all the growth and earnings for all the years the account exists. Take advantage of it!

THE NEW ROTH IRA

Also effective in 1998 is the new Roth IRA. Unlike the traditional IRA which may be funded with *before*-tax contributions (depending upon AGI), Roth IRA contributions are always made with *after*-tax dollars (meaning you have already paid income taxes on the money you use to fund the Roth IRA).

Like the traditional IRA, you are not taxed each year on the growth and earnings of your Roth IRA investments. Withdrawals from the traditional IRA, you will recall, are taxed at your ordinary income tax rates at the time you make them (i.e. in retirement). Unlike the traditional IRA, *all* withdrawals from the

Roth IRA, including all the earnings, are yours tax-free, *forever*! As long as you are at least 59-1/2 years old and the money has been in the account for at least five years, you will *never* be taxed on anything you withdraw from your Roth IRA! The Roth IRA is one of the best opportunities for individual investors to come down the pike in years!

All the same IRA rules apply to the Roth IRA. There is a 10% penalty (plus taxes on earnings) for early withdrawal. Loans are not permitted, but you may make penalty-free withdrawals for college education and up to $10,000 for a first-time home purchase. The maximum annual IRA contribution is $2,000 per person. (You can contribute to either the traditional IRA, or to a Roth IRA, or to both, as long your total contribution for the year does not exceed $2,000). Unlike the traditional IRA you can make contributions to a Roth IRA well beyond age 70-1/2 and there is no age at which you are required to begin taking distributions from your Roth IRA.

Depending upon your income level you can convert a traditional IRA to a Roth IRA by taking the money out of the traditional IRA and rolling it over to the Roth IRA. Although the 10% early withdrawal penalty is waived for these rollovers, you will have to pay any income taxes due on the money from the traditional IRA, in the year of conversion. If the conversion occurred in 1998 (and only in 1998) you were able to spread out the payment of the income taxes over four years instead of one. If you make too much money you cannot convert a traditional IRA (or even contribute) to a Roth IRA.

Which IRA is right you? Does paying the income taxes for a Roth IRA conversion make sense financially? A "Millionaire in the Making" with a time horizon of five years or more will almost always be better off with the Roth IRA. As far as the conversion is concerned, the time horizon is important but so is the size of your existing traditional IRA account. Do you have the ability to pay the income taxes and the sufficient time to grow your investments to recover the taxes you must pay? Your tax advisor or your financial advisor has software to make these comparisons and can help you make such decisions. Generally speaking, it is better to pay taxes on today's money than on tomorrow's money.

OTHER IMPORTANT CHANGES FOR INVESTORS

As a side note, the same legislation which liberalized the traditional IRA and created the new Roth IRA also created the new Educational IRA. This allows parents and grandparents to help pay for the cost of a child's college education by allowing contributions of $500 a year to an Educational IRA account established for a child under the age of 18. Earnings grow tax-free, and withdrawals are tax-free and penalty-free (as long as the money is used to pay for tuition, room and board).

The legislation, which is called the Taxpayers Relief Act of 1997, also lowered the capital gains tax rate from 28% to 20%. This of course only applies to capital gains earned on investments held outside of tax-advantaged accounts, and the lower rate is available only for investments which are held for 18 months or longer.

VARIABLE ANNUITIES

Once you've taken full and complete advantage of workplace retirement savings plans by deferring as much as your salary as you possibly can, and then you make your annual $2,000 IRA contributions, where else can you turn for tax-advantaged wealth-building?

To variable annuities. A variable annuity is an insurance contract which allows you to invest in mutual funds and have your earnings grow tax-deferred. It is often described as "mutual fund investing inside an insurance wrapper." Although a variable annuity is not a life insurance contract, it is a contract with an insurance company, and this is why the IRS allows the tax-advantaged growth of earnings. Virtually every mutual fund company has teamed up with an insurance company to offer variable annuities to investors, and billions of dollars have poured into them over the years.

Variable annuities are very flexible. You may fund the contract with as much money as you like whenever you like, and you can set up as many variable annuities as you like (though it may be easier to keep funding existing ones).

You can invest in lump sums, or you can invest systematically. Minimums apply just as they do in mutual fund investing.

You can transfer or rollover qualified retirement money into a variable annuity, or you can use after-tax dollars (though each type requires a separate contract). If you rollover money from a tax-qualified plan, the same IRS rules apply to the variable annuity as they did to the original plan (10% early-withdrawal if less than age 59-1/2 on top of any ordinary income taxes which may be due). If you use after-tax dollars instead, these IRS rules are not applicable.

There are two phases to every variable annuity. The first is the accumulation phase during which you make contributions and allow your money to grow. You choose how to allocate and reallocate your investment dollars among the various mutual funds available within the contract. Because they are part of the insurance contract they are kept separate from the mutual fund companies' regular family of funds, and they are called subaccounts instead of mutual funds.

The portfolios of the subaccounts are often managed by the same professionals who manage the portfolios of the regular mutual funds. The subaccounts have their own performance results which may or may not mirror the performance results of their corresponding mutual fund counterparts. The subaccounts generally have higher operating expenses, and the insurance company will have its own administrative and insurance-related expenses on top of these. The offsetting advantage presumably is the tax-deferral on investment earnings, and any pay-out guarantees provided by the insurance company regarding the account should the contract owner die.

The second phase in the annuity contract is the annuitization phase during which the insurance company pays you according to the choices you make at the time you begin annuitization, if and when you ever annuitize the account. An annuity is designed to enable you to receive predetermined periodic payments, much like an employer's pension plan. You make the decisions as to how you want to receive the payments, and depending upon the value of your account at the time of annuitization the insurance company will calculate the payment amounts based upon your choices.

The amounts will vary based upon the choices. You can tell them you want to receive payments for the rest of your life. Once you die they stop (and the insurance company keeps the balance of the account, if any). Or you can tell them you want payments for the rest of your life, and once you die, you want your spouse to continue receiving payments until your spouse dies (and the insurance company keeps the balance of the account, if any). Or you can say you want the company to make payments for a period certain, for ten, fifteen, or twenty years. If you die during this time the payments will continue to designated beneficiaries for the period certain.

Annuitization is like flipping a switch: you are in the accumulation phase and all the money is yours to invest as you desire, until you flip the switch and enter the annuitization phase during which you receive a payout according to the choices you make with the insurance company at the time you elect to begin annuitization.

At this point you no longer have direct access to your money, only to the annuity payment schedule you arranged with the insurance company. The insurance company is contractually bound to honor the payment schedule, and once the commitment is fulfilled the contract is terminated.

Depending upon the payment schedule you select, and how long you live if applicable, it's possible to receive far more, or far less, than your original investment and the growth of the investment.

Obviously the decisions you make about annuitization are extremely important and require a great deal of consideration.

Although some contracts force annuitization at a certain age, at age 85 or 95 for example, most people never annuitize. By remaining in the accumulation phase the money is always yours to control, and you can always get your money out whenever you want by surrendering the contract. Although most variable annuities do not charge up-front commissions to get into them, they do have surrender charges which operate just like the Contingent Deferred Sales Charges on Class B mutual fund shares. The percentage is higher in earlier years, declines over time, and disappears entirely after the seventh or eighth year. They often allow annual withdrawals free of surrender charges for up to 10% of your principal, but anything beyond the 10% withdrawal will be assessed a surrender charge.

All of the details of a variable annuity are spelled out in the prospectus which, as always, you should carefully review prior to making any investments. Variable annuities are a popular tax-advantaged investment vehicle as evidenced by the billions of dollars which continue to flow into them every year. They may or may not be right for you in your own wealth-building efforts but you won't know unless you spend some time learning more about them. A professional advisor can help you.

OTHER TAX-ADVANTAGED INSURANCE PRODUCTS

In addition to variable annuities there are other insurance products you can use to fund your retirement years. Theses are primarily life insurance policies which provide for tax-advantaged accumulation and growth of investments coupled with pure life insurance. They are more complex in design and execution, and generally require a greater financial commitment, than variable annuity contracts. But because they may enable you to fund your retirement with money that is completely tax-free to you, they deserve mention here. Ask your financial advisor and the insurance companies for more information, including policy illustrations.

THE QUICKEST WAY TO BECOMING A MILLIONAIRE

You can accelerate your goal of becoming a millionaire by taking full advantage of tax-advantaged investing. Keep in mind that if you are less than 59-1/2 years of age and you take money out of a tax-qualified plan, the IRS will hit you with a 10% early-withdrawal penalty (also known as a premature distribution penalty) on top of ordinary taxes you may have to pay If, however, your millionaire goal takes you past age 59-1/2, then all else being equal, tax-advantaged investing will get you there the quickest.

Deferring taxation on the earnings and growth of your investments allows the miracle of compounding to work to your greater benefit because the compounding occurs on a larger base of capital, one that is not reduced by taxes year in and year out.

Whether it is through a retirement savings plan at work, a retirement savings plan set up through your own business, Individual Retirement Accounts (IRAs), variable annuities, life insurance, or any combination of the above, do what you can to protect your Millionaire Investment Fund from the Millionaire's sccond greatest enemy - Taxes - by taking full advantage of the tax-advantaged investing opportunities available to you.

Do what you can to protect your Millionaire Investment Fund from the Millionaire's second greatest enemy - Taxes - by taking full advantage of the tax-advantaged investing opportunities available to you.

You can accelerate your goal of becoming a millionaire by taking full advantage of tax-advantaged investing.

A GRANDFATHER'S ADVICE TO THE ASPIRING MILLIONAIRE

"If you can't afford to pay cash for it, you can't afford it." This loving, common sense advice comes from a loving, common sense grandfather who is perplexed by people's seemingly insatiable desire to acquire material possessions at any cost, including going into debt to do it.

We all have relatives who lived through the Great Depression of the 1930s. This is our last frugal generation, coming from the pre-debt, pre-installment-plan era. Easy payment plans were few and far between. Credit cards did not exist. If you wanted something you paid cash for it. If you didn't have the cash, you had to save up for it. There were no alternatives. Talk to anyone who survived the Great Depression and you'll discover they adhered to their advice all of their lives. The advice serves well in every generation. If you can't afford to pay cash for it, you can't afford it.

Today's consumption-oriented society is very different from the savings-oriented society of recent generations. Today we live in a society where instant gratification isn't quick enough. We want it all and we want it now. And we're willing to go into debt to get it. Each year billions of dollars are spent on advertising to seduce us and induce us into parting with our money to buy things which promise to make us look better, feel better, and live better than we ever lived before. And we don't have to wait until we have the cash to do it. We can mortgage our future by digging into future earnings to pay for all the stuff we want to have today.

YOU'RE GETTING CHEATED TWENTY CENTS ON THE DOLLAR

When you go shopping you find two items exactly identical in every way but one - price. Side by side both items are the same, but one is priced $100 and the other $120. Who in their right mind would choose the higher-priced item?

Yet that's exactly the choice you make when you buy on credit. The reason you make it is because you must pay cash up front to get the $100 price. If you're willing to pay $120, you can have it without paying cash up front. You can have the item today as long as you agree to pay $20 more for it, $20 more than it's worth. You need only to promise to pay for it eventually, at the ridiculously-inflated price, and it's yours. Why save up the cash when you can buy using credit cards?

If the credit card has an annual interest rate of 20%, it means you're paying 20% more for your item because the finance charge of 20% is added to the cost of the purchase. It means, in essence, that you are getting cheated twenty cents on the dollar, and the greatest tragedy of all is that you're the one cheating yourself. If it takes longer than a year to pay off the charge, the price you paid for that item continues to go up due to prolonged financing charges. The miracle of compounding kicks in, to the bank's great advantage and to your great detriment.

It's called consumer debt and nationally it adds up to hundreds of billions of dollars. It's a national malady. It's an addiction of epic proportions. Banks rake in billions of dollars of revenue from consumers who are willing to pay 20% more for everything they buy on credit. The interest and finance charges you pay to a bank is money that could be going toward your own financial independence.

That's right. Buying on credit means you choose to give your money to a bank and help *it* - the bank - become financially independent, instead of to you for your own financial independence. Even if it has become the American Way, it's just plain stupid. It is tragic that it has become the American Way. It was not always the American Way. Ask your grandmother or grandfather. Consumer debt is a sad testament to the tragedy that is Instant Gratification At Any Price, which has seemingly become our new national anthem.

DEBT IS A FOUR-LETTER WORD THAT MILLIONAIRES DO NOT SPEAK

Debt is a four-letter word, meaning it's distasteful, even abhorrent. Avoid debt like the plague that it is. Debt is like a huge albatross hanging around the neck of a "Millionaire in the Making". It's like driving with one foot on the gas pedal and the other on the brake. Debt puts a huge drag on your wealth-building program.

All it takes is the self-discipline and self-control necessary to break any negative habit, and debting is a negative habit at best, and an outright addiction at worst. You begin breaking the habit by reprogramming your mind until you are absolutely convinced that becoming a Millionaire is your most important financial goal, and the burden of debt is one of the biggest obstacles to achieving your goal. Do whatever it takes to overcome this obstacle!

HOW TO GET OUT OF DEBT

You can begin immediately by making and honoring this commitment: "Just for today I will not debt." This will stop debting's downward spiral from getting any worse.

Then get this book: *How to Get Out of Debt, Stay Out of Debt & Live Prosperously (Based on the Proven Principles and*

Techniques of Debtors Anonymous) by Jerrold Mundis. It is one of the best books ever written on the subject, and it will deliver what the title promises. Mundis, a self-proclaimed recovered debtor, takes you step by step through the debt recovery process.

As overwhelming a task it may appear to you, you do not have to sacrifice your life to bail yourself out of debt. You merely design a debt repayment plan that you can live with, and then honor it month in and month out. Your creditors may not be able to live with your repayment plan and may harass you accordingly, but if you are unable to honor and live with the repayment plan they demand, they're going to harass you anyway.

The book provides all the details you need to succeed and if you stick with the program outlined in the book, no matter how long it may take, you will emerge and remain debt-free.

HOW TO WORK ON TWO GOALS SIMULTANEOUSLY

You only have a certain amount of dollars coming in each month. How do you reconcile your need to save money and your need to pay off your debts?

The conventional wisdom says that you should pay off your credit cards first. You're being charged 18% to 22% a year on these debts, and if your investments only deliver an average annual return of 10%, it only makes sense to pay off your debts first. The conventional wisdom will suggest you should even use money earmarked for savings to pay off debts. Paying off your debts as quickly as possible frees up the 18% to 22% in finance charges you are paying, and once the debts are gone you can put the money to work for you.

Don't follow the "conventional" wisdom! Reread chapters *The Secret Formula for Becoming a Millionaire* and *Three Magic Words That Will Help You Become a Millionaire.* Debt repayment, including finance charges (whatever the interest rate), comes from Spend dollars, not Save dollars. Spend dollars are what's left over after taking Save dollars off the top of your income. Nothing interferes with Save dollars, remember?

Not all credit cards charge an annual interest rate of 20%. Many offer you a low teaser rate of 5.9% to 9.9% to induce you to open an account and transfer existing balances. Then, typically after six months or so, the rate then jumps up to the normal rate which will be prorated monthly and assessed against the entire outstanding balance on the account. The normal annual rate usually falls between 18% and 22%.

The conventional wisdom also says to prioritize your debts by the annual rate of interest you're being charged, and pay off the highest rate balances first, then the next highest, and so on. This bit of wisdom is okay to follow if it appeals to you.

On the other hand, even though this idea makes sense financially, you may struggle with it emotionally if larger balance debts carry lower interest rates. In this case, it may be psychologically advantageous to pay off the lower balance debts regardless of the interest rates. As the debts disappear you will feel like you're making progress, appreciate that your efforts produce results, and stay motivated to continue and perhaps even accelerate your efforts and results.

STICK TO CASH

All future purchases are to be made strictly with cash. Working strictly with cash means you have to set priorities for your Spend dollars. You have to decide what is truly important enough to you to part with your hard-earned cash.

Remember the words of your much beloved, very wise grandparent: "If you can't afford to pay cash for it, you can't afford it." If you live by this advice and make it the rule in your life, you will become a Millionaire much faster than the majority of people who go into debt in order to satisfy their desire for instant gratification. Call it Delayed Gratification. Once you are a Millionaire you will have plenty of cash for the rest of your life to buy all the things you want.

If you can't afford it today, you should not be buying it today, no matter how badly you want it. If you don't have the cash, you can't afford it!

There's one exception on the use of debt. Use it to finance the purchase of a home, (which is covered in the next chapter).

"If you can't afford to pay cash for it, you can't afford it."

If you live by this advice and make it the rule in your life, you will become a Millionaire much faster.

Avoid debt like the plague that it is. Debt puts a huge drag on your wealth-building program. It's like driving with one foot on the gas pedal and the other on the brake.

Once you are a Millionaire you will have plenty of cash for the rest of your life to buy all the things you want.

THE ORIGINAL AMERICAN DREAM

Becoming a Millionaire is an American Dream which is shared by millions but the Original American Dream is to own your own home. How does this dream fit into your dream of becoming a Millionaire?

Owning your own home should be one of your first objectives on your road to Financial Independence, and taking on debt to finance the purchase of your home is the major (if only) exception to the No-Debt rule.

It's tough to save up the money to pay cash outright for the purchase of a home, so a bank will gladly step in to help you - in exchange for the thousands and thousands of dollars in interest it will collect from you over the years.

Home ownership has long been the "American Dream", and our government has long encouraged it and assisted us in achieving it. It does this by providing financial incentives in the form of tax benefits.

Every year on your income tax return you'll be able to deduct the interest you pay on your loan and the taxes you pay on your property. Also, as you make improvements to your property, you can add these costs to your purchase price which serves to reduce your taxable basis when you sell.

There are other important reasons for owning your own home, like the peace of mind, personal satisfaction, independence and security you'll experience from owning your piece of the "American Dream."

You'll always need a place to live, so the basic choice becomes either Rent or Own. When you pay rent, you have absolutely nothing to show for it except rent receipts. And you'll have to pay rent for the rest of your life.

In contrast, by choosing to own, your monthly mortgage payments bring you closer and closer to 100% ownership of your own home. The difference between the market value of the property (what you'd get it for it if you sold it at any given time) and the amount of money you owe on the loan, is called *equity*. Equity represents the percentage of the market value that belongs to you.

In addition, Real Estate is considered an *appreciating* asset, meaning it tends to go up in value over time. As you learned earlier, it's good to invest your money in appreciating assets! There are no guarantees on that appreciation, but historically the odds are in your favor, particularly over long periods of time. The longer the time you own it, the greater the likelihood of appreciation in value.

So two things typically occur as you're making your monthly mortgage payments: as time goes on, you are increasing your equity in an asset that is also growing in value itself.

These payments will eventually end and you'll never have to make them again! When you consider the fact that housing expense usually represents anywhere from 25% to 33% of monthly income, think about how much that will help your Financial Independence plan when it goes away. This is a major reason people take out the usual thirty-year loan to buy a home, and then make extra payments on the principal to pay it off as soon as possible.

Keep in mind that when you pay rent, the odds are pretty high you're helping to pay that property-owner's mortgage on the property you're renting. Would you like the money you pay for housing to go toward building someone else's wealth, or toward building your own wealth?

Learn what you need to learn and do what you need to do to fulfill the Original American Dream for yourself. Owning your own home fits in well with the other American Dream of becoming a Millionaire.

You'll always need a place to live, so the basic choice becomes either Rent or Own. When you pay rent, you have absolutely nothing to show for it except rent receipts. And you'll have to pay rent for the rest of your life.

When you consider the fact that housing expense usually represents 25% to 33% of monthly income, would you like the money you pay for housing to go toward building someone else's wealth, or toward building your own wealth?

Owning your own home fits in well with the other American Dream of becoming a Millionaire.

PROTECTING YOUR WEALTH

The focus of this book has been on building wealth. Although this is not a book on financial planning, you need to know that *building* wealth is not enough.

You must also *protect* your wealth too. You need to educate yourself and make decisions about Taxes, Insurance and Estate Planning. The concepts are easy to understand, but the solutions and products are complex. Your financial advisor may be able to help you and/or refer you to specialists. Don't hesitate to pay for the services of professional advisors who specialize in helping people protect their wealth.

TAXES

Remembering that a Millionaire's second greatest enemy is Taxes, do what you can to protect your wealth from attack by taxation. You learned about tax-advantaged investing, but you can do even more to protect your wealth by finding a tax specialist to advise you on other strategies and tactics designed to lower your overall tax burden.

It is one thing to find a professional to prepare your tax return, but it is an altogether different thing when you find a professional who also takes a proactive role by regularly advising you on specific actions you can take to minimize your tax bill. If such advice is not volunteered by your current tax preparer, ask for it anyway, and consider looking for a proactive tax advisor.

INSURANCE

Health Insurance protects your wealth from harm due to medical expenses incurred as a result of the professional attention required to maintain or restore your health. Medical costs have risen substantially faster than the historical rate of inflation. Don't gamble with your health, and don't gamble your wealth on your health.

Life Insurance will protect your wealth from harm due to the possibility of your premature death. You can't take your money with you when you die, but you can protect the wealth you worked so hard to build for the continued benefit and enjoyment of the loved ones you leave behind. Adequate life insurance replaces the present and future income your family will lose as a result of your death. If this income is not replaced, they may need to tap into (and perhaps deplete) the wealth you've built in order to survive financially. Also, if you've built enough wealth, estate taxes may have to be paid upon your death. Life Insurance is often used to provide your loved ones with the funds necessary to pay the taxes without having to liquidate assets (including perhaps the family home) to pay the tax bill.

Disability Income Insurance protects your wealth from harm due to the possibility you become temporarily or permanently disabled. In some cases the financial impact of a disability may be worse than death! Becoming disabled means your income-producing ability is compromised, but unlike death your living expenses continue (and may even increase). You may be forced to liquidate and deplete assets to survive financially, and the quality of your life deteriorates accordingly. Your odds of becoming temporarily disabled are usually greater than the odds of dying, and the odds increase (worsen) with age.

Long-Term Care Insurance protects your wealth from harm due to the possibility you require long-term health care due to a sudden accident, protracted illness, or other long-term mental or physical impairment which prevents you from taking care of yourself. Skilled or semi-skilled care whether in a nursing home or in your own home is extremely expensive, and long-term care insurance is designed to help you pay these costs without sacrificing all of your wealth.

Property Insurance protects your physical assets (autos, homes, etc.) from physical damage and loss, and Liability Insurance protects all of your assets (physical and financial) from third-party claims. If the insurance you carry is insufficient to satisfy damage losses and claims, you will have to tap into your wealth to satisfy them.

Protect your wealth by carrying adequate Insurance. Insurance premiums should not be viewed as an expense but as an investment designed to protect your wealth.

ESTATE PLANNING

The first thing you need to do is to draft your will. The purpose of a legally valid will is to state your intentions regarding the distribution of your wealth in the event of your death, and if applicable, to name the individuals you prefer to serve as guardians of your minor children. If you die without a legally valid will, all of these decisions will be made for you according to existing state statutes. Would you like to make these important decisions yourself or have the state make them for you? Draft your will!

When you die your survivors must settle your estate and distribute your wealth, which may involve the probate court. In order to transfer property at your death they may need to either "prove" your intentions by producing your will and/or trust document, or if there is no will ask the court to direct the transfers and settle the estate.

Probate is time-consuming and expensive, and is avoidable through the proper titling of ownership of your assets, and/or through the creation of a trust in which you name and empower trustees to act on your behalf in the event of your incapacity to act (including your death).

Estate planning can help minimize or even eliminate estate taxes which may be due upon your death.

Proper estate planning protects your wealth and deserves your time and attention while you are alive. Be sure to invest some money and hire an estate-planning attorney to review your decisions and any legal documents you may have drafted yourself.

***Building* wealth is not enough. You must also *protect* your wealth too.**

Find a tax specialist to advise you on strategies and tactics to lower your overall tax burden.

Protect your wealth by carrying adequate Insurance. Insurance premiums should not be viewed as an expense but as an investment designed to protect your wealth.

Proper estate planning protects your wealth, and it deserves your time and attention while you are alive.

THE JOURNEY OF A MILLION DOLLARS BEGINS WITH THIS

The ancient Chinese proverb that "A journey of a thousand miles begins with the first step" can be applied to any goal in your life, including your goal of becoming a Millionaire.

The journey of a million dollars begins with the first dollar. The sooner you start, the sooner you arrive.

You already harbor the dream in your mind and the desire in your heart. This book shows you a way to make your dream come alive, keep it alive, and turn it into reality. It is not the only way, and it may or may not be the best way. It is a way that has worked for others who have gone before you with the same dream, desire, and goal. What is possible for others is possible for you.

Yet there are no guarantees. No one can know what the future holds. The one thing we both know for certain is that your goal cannot become reality unless you take action. The journey of a million dollars begins with the first dollar. So take the first step, and then the next, and then the next. It is a long-term proposition, so be patient and have a long-term perspective. Save that first dollar, and then the next, and then the next.

Keep converting a dollar of income into a dollar of capital. Every dollar you put to work for you is another dollar you will never have to work for again. With the miracle of compounding, every dollar you convert to capital brings you *more* than one dollar closer to your goal!

When you get discouraged, as you sometimes will, return to this book for inspiration and encouragement. Return to this chapter. If nothing else, remember this one very important fact:

YOU ARE CLOSER TODAY TO BECOMING A MILLIONAIRE THAN YOU WERE YESTERDAY

You are an Aspiring Millionaire. If you are doing what you know you should be doing, it means you are saving and growing your money. It means every day brings you closer and closer to your goal. You are closer to being a Millionaire today than you were yesterday.

You truly are a "Millionaire in the Making".

So keep taking the next step, but remember to enjoy the journey.

I wish you well, and I am confident you will succeed.

You are an Aspiring Millionaire.

The journey of a million dollars begins with the first dollar. Save that first dollar, and then the next, and then the next.

The sooner you start, the sooner you arrive.

You are closer to being a Millionaire today than you were yesterday.

You truly are a "Millionaire in the Making."

Enjoy the journey.

THE ROAD NOT TAKEN

The sad truth is most people do not become financially independent, and even less become millionaires.

But you are not like most people, are you?

If you are to become financially independent, it should be obvious to you that you need to do something different than what most people are doing.

You need to travel a different road than the one most people travel.

I leave you with these immortal words, penned by Robert Frost in his poem *The Road Not Taken*:

> Two roads diverged in a wood, and I--
> I took the one less traveled by,
> And that has made all the difference.
> ROBERT FROST

You are not like most people, are you?

Remember the immortal words of Robert Frost, from his poem *The Road Not Taken*:

> **Two roads diverged in a wood, and I--**
> **I took the one less traveled by,**
> **And that has made all the difference.**

AFTERWORD

I'd love to hear from you. Has this book helped you in any way? Is there anything that could be done to make this book better and more accessible to those most in need of the information?

Do you have a success story you would like to share?

Please send your written comments to me:

Ed Dzwonkowski
c/o Great Spirit Publishing Company
P.O. Box 5520
Huntington Beach, California 92646

Or e-mail me via Great Spirit Publishing's web site:

www.greatspiritpub.com

BIBLIOGRAPHY

Interesting Reading for Aspiring Millionaires

Think and Grow Rich by Napolean Hill. Fawcett Crest/Ballantine, 1990 (latest printing). A timeless classic on the laws of financial success, to be read again and again, absorbed, and applied to your own financial goals.

The Richest Man in Babylon by George S. Clason. New American Library, 1997 (latest printing). Another timeless classic. Written as an interesting and entertaining parable, it conveys the basic concepts of financial planning and disciplined wealth-building.

The Wealthy Barber: Everyone's Common-Sense Guide to Becoming Financially Independent by David Chilton. Prima Publishing, 1997 (latest printing). Another interesting and entertaining parable, it is the story of a barber who dispenses homespun advice about building wealth and becoming financially independent.

The Millionaire Next Door: The Surprising Secrets of America's Wealthy by Thomas J. Stanley and William D. Danko. Longstreet Press, 1996. Having researched the wealthy in this country for many years, the authors share their findings on how ordinary Americans get rich and stay rich. Interesting reading, you will be surprised and inspired.

Your Money or Your Life: Transforming Your Relationship With Money And Achieving Financial Independence by Joe Dominguez and Vicki Robin. Penguin Books, 1993. The only issue I take with this otherwise fine work is the authors' viewpoint on the importance and impact of inflation, the advice to steer clear of professional financial advisors and do it all on your own, and the advice to invest all of your savings in long-term U.S. treasury and U.S. government agency bonds. Professional disagreement aside, I highly recommend this book because you will learn much about money and becoming financially independent.

On Eliminating Debt

How to Get Out of Debt, Stay Out of Debt & Live Prosperously: Based Upon the Proven Principles and Techniques of Debtors Anonymous by Jerrold Mundis. Bantam Books, 1990. Perhaps the best book on the subject ever written. The author writes from personal experience and is friendly, engaging, and supportive.

On Saving Money

The Tightwad Gazette: *Promoting Thrift as a Viable Alternative Lifestyle* by Amy Dacyczyn. Random House, 1993. Labeled a "tireless advocate of voluntary simplicity," the author has published The Tightwad Gazette newsletter for years through which she and her readers share tips and techniques for living well on less. This book and the two subsequent volumes (published by Villard Books in 1995 and 1997 respectively) are collections of articles culled from the monthly newsletter. Something for everybody.

On Earning Money

Earn What You Deserve: How To Stop Underearning & Start Thriving by Jerrold Mundis. Bantam Books, 1996. By the same author featured above, he discusses under-earning and what to do about it. It might be an eye-opener for you. It can help you change your thoughts and feelings about your relationship with money.

On Finding Fulfilling Employment

What Color Is Your Parachute by Richard Nelson Bolles. Ten Speed Press, updated annually. With millions of copies in print, this is a preeminent classic about finding your way in terms of matching your talents, interests, skills, and experiences with income-producing possibilities. Be prepared for some serious introspection and self-analysis, then follow the steps to personal and financial fulfillment.

Who's Hiring Who? How to Find That Job Fast by Richard Lathrop. Ten Speed Press, 1989 (latest edition). One of the better job-hunting guides on the market, it should serve you well as you search for your next job opportunity, which hopefully makes you happier and results in your earning more money than you've ever earned before!

ORDER FORM

We encourage you to support your local bookseller. If your local bookseller does not currently stock this book, ask him or her to special order it for you. If you prefer, you may phone, fax, or mail your order directly to us, or order online through our Internet web site:

Great Spirit Publishing Company
P.O. Box 5520
Huntington Beach, California 92646
Voice/Fax: (714) 969-6806
www.greatspiritpub.com

Name ____

Address ____

City, State, Zip ____________________________________

Quantity: _______ x $19.95 each = _________

California residents add 7.75% sales tax: _________

Shipping ($3.50 for the first book, $1.50 for each additional) _________

TOTAL: _________

❑ Check enclosed. ❑ Charge my credit card:

❑ MasterCard ❑ Visa ❑ American Express ❑ Discover

Card number: ___________________________ Exp. date _________

Signature: _______________________________________